Picass

D0615287

A STUDY OF HIS WORK BY
FRANK ELGAR

A BIOGRAPHICAL STUDY BY
ROBERT MAILLARD

TRANSLATED FROM THE FRENCH BY
FRANCIS SCARFE

Frederick A. Praeger

NEW YORK

OUR WARMEST THANKS ARE OFFERED TO
M. JAIME SABARTÉS,
MME LOUISE LEIRIS AND M. D-H. KAHNWEILER,
FOR THE NUMEROUS WAYS IN WHICH THEY HAVE HELPED
IN THE PREPARATION OF THIS BOOK

WE PARTICULARLY THANK
PABLO PICASSO
FOR HIS ENCOURAGEMENT OF THIS PROJECT
AND THE INTEREST HE HAS SHOWN IN OUR WORK
AND OFFER HIM OUR GRATITUDE FOR
HIS INVALUABLE SUPPORT

WE THANK THE PUBLISHERS AND EDITORS OF CERCLE D'ART
FOR THE USE OF THE EKTACHROME OF THE
PORTRAIT OF AMBROISE VOLLARD
MR PAUL ROSENBERG OF NEW YORK
AND MR SIEGFRIED ROSENGART OF LUCERNE
AS WELL AS THE OTHER COLLECTORS AND AMATEURS
WHO ENABLED US TO PHOTOGRAPH THE WORKS
IN THEIR POSSESSION

FIRST PUBLISHED IN THE UNITED STATES OF AMERICA IN 1956
BY FREDERICK A. PRAEGER, INC.
150 EAST 52 STREET, NEW YORK 22
ALL RIGHTS RESERVED
LIBRARY OF CONGRESS CATALOG CARD NO. 56-10253

COLOR PHOTOGRAPHY BY
BARNEY BERNSTEIN, BOSTON, MASS.
WALTER DRAYER, ZURICH; JACQUES ELSER, PARIS
FRANCIS G. MAYER, NEW YORK
THE ENGRAVINGS WERE MADE BY
THE PERROT AND GRISET STUDIOS
AND CLICHÉS UNION
DESIGNED BY MARCEL JACNO
PRINTED IN GERMANY

FOREWORD

WE feel it is necessary to point out why and how this new work on Picasso differs from all others. Our aim has been to offer the public a complete account as well as, wherever possible, an explanation of the work, the life and the man about whom so much has already been written. An examination of the numerous books devoted to this artist makes it clear that they all deal with some aspects of his temperament, some particular part of his output, one or several phases of his career. But it is the entire Picasso, sixty years of his creative activity, that is presented in this volume, by means of a text whose lucidity we hope will be apparent to all, and a large number of illustrations that could not have been more carefully selected.

Frank Elgar has undertaken the task of describing and interpreting the artist's works, and Robert Maillard that of writing a biography, both working side by side and using the same chronological method, which is the only one capable of clearly revealing the extremely complex nature of such a fertile and many-sided artist. In order to give this study the scope it deserves we have made a point of reproducing all the works analysed or mentioned in the text. Besides the large number of six-colour or black-and-white illustrations which accompany the text as closely as possible, we have added an illustrated catalogue of the artist's principal pictures, set out in chronological order. The reader will also find, at the end of the book, a check list of paintings, drawings, sculptures and ceramics by Picasso to be found in the various museums in Europe, which is now compiled for the first time.

FLYING DOVE. 9 JULY 1950. LITHOGRAPH, 21⅝″ × 27⅝″.

Pablo Ruiz Picasso was born at Malaga, Andalusia, on the 25th of October 1881. It is sometimes said, but without evidence, that his mother, Maria Picasso, was descended from an old Majorcan family of goldsmiths. His father, José Ruiz Blasco, is now known to be of New Castilian and not Basque descent. When the critics noticed a few years ago that Picasso's surname has an Italian ring about it, and that there is no double s in Spanish, the rumour spread that his ancestors on his mother's side were perhaps of Italian origin. Colour was given to this legend, and it became all the more acceptable, when it was found that in the nineteenth century there was a fairly well-known painter in Genoa, called Matteo Picasso. But it is as well to remember that the ss was used in Old Castilian writings; thus there is no need to suppose that one of the artist's ancestors migrated to Italy, or that his name was perhaps modified from Picazo to that form which is now a household word.

At the time of Pablo's birth the family was living at 36 (now 15), Plaza de la Merced, on the third floor. Don José was teaching painting and drawing at the School of Arts and Crafts in Malaga, which served the province. He had managed to establish himself in a modest way as a painter of flower-pieces and still-lifes with game and wildfowl, and was not without patrons.

Pigeons were his favourite subject. Those pigeons were to play an unusual

6

It has been claimed that art is an expression of society. This has sometimes been the case, but Picasso's art is that of a particular man. The one cannot be understood without the other. Whether in painting, engraving, sculpture, or ceramics, the manifold and ever-changing work of Picasso is in his own image. A powerful man, of exceptional temperament, energy and virility; passionate but self-contained, ardent yet not very sensual, restless and yet attached to the good things of life, a man who stifles his own doubts by means of an incredible frenzy of creation; sincere when he least appears to be, and unreliable when outwardly at his most sincere; mocking, insolent and proud in public, yet unaffected, warm-hearted and jovial in private life; sceptical and suspicious, full of that masculine uneasiness which is commonly found in souls of superior mettle and whom it stimulates to action instead of throwing them into despair; a prodigious creator yet at heart a fierce negator, Picasso has sent his blasphemies echoing down our century and filled it with his sarcasms and challenges; and yet the same rebel can be a good husband, a passionate lover, a tender and entrancing parent; but all this, it is to be admitted, he does with neither faith nor constancy, but with a kind of cruel gentleness and an extravagant dissipation of himself.

The many photographs of Picasso portray him either in the

part in young Pablo's life, as the boy refused to go to school unless he were allowed to take one of his father's birds into the classroom. In this way Pablo was able to while away his time by drawing during lessons. From about the age of seven he was never without a pencil in his hand, and was already arousing his parents' admiration. His sister Lolita and his girl-cousins used to delight in challenging him to draw the most unlikely things, such as a dog, a cock or a donkey, with the

stipulation that he must begin at such and such a point. Thus one would want him to begin with the ear, another with the paw. It was not without a certain satisfaction that Picasso responded to all these demands, for he saw little point in obeying the traditional rules when his own skill enabled him to snatch success out of difficulty.

1891—The Malaga province Museum of which José Ruiz Blasco was the curator now had to close down. Pablo's

struggling obscurity of his early career or else at the height of his fame. They show a thick-set body, a broad forehead, a sardonic mouth, a thick nose, restless eyes, and remarkably strong and nimble hands. Those hands were specially designed for kneading, shaping and modelling, busy and impatient hands born for giving outline, volume and density to everything they touch, and for drawing living forms out of inert matter, transforming the original clay into a host of plastic creations; they are plebeian but delicate hands, active and free, capable of thinking and wishing and feeling for themselves, when the heart is cold and the brain is weary; hands that can unleash a devil's anger or a vampire's craving only a few seconds after they have untied a child's hair-ribbon or stroked some lost dog. When the eyes see nothing but surface appearances, those hands have enough flair in their touch to lay hold on the world and tear apart the veil of time, and probe the secrets of the earth and the myths of primitive man. Artists such as Monet, who are all retina, have failed to do more than reproduce the outward aspects of nature. Matisse saw nothing but its surfaces and saturated them with colour, while Fernand Léger knew how to bring out its dominant lines and structures. But Picasso has explored both the contours and inwardness of things with his own hands, measured their weights and volumes, defined them in space, in a series of experiments beyond

father was thus obliged to make a vital decision in order to provide for his family. He decided to move house from Malaga to Corunna, where he was given a teaching appointment at the Da Guarda Institute, which had secondary status. The removal took place in mid-September and with some misgiving, for as an Andalusian José did not relish the damp climate awaiting him in the Atlantic port. Pablo was benefiting from his father's advice and working feverishly. The boy was so enthusiastic that in 1894 Don José gave up painting altogether and solemnly presented all his colours and brushes to his son. He sensed that the boy would succeed where he had failed. And indeed the young Picasso had already picked up a sufficiently competent technique to paint such canvases as the Two Old Men and The Barefooted Girl.

July 1895—The whole family went to Malaga for the holidays, after which at the end of September they

NTRANCE TO THE BULL-RING. 1901. PASTEL ON CARDBOARD, 11″ × 11″.

the scope of mere optics. His fingers have felt all the hollows and contours of the world, and even if he came close to reducing it to chaos he has held the universe in the palm of his hand, just as he has held man, if only as a hollow skull.

He was already drawing and painting at thirteen, and had reached his artistic maturity by the age of twenty. His early works need not detain us, though they are as breath-taking as some concerto played by an infant prodigy in short trousers. He showed a disconcerting command of the pencil by 1900, when Berthe Weill bought three of his sketches of *corridas* during his first visit to Paris. He returned to Paris the next year, when he exhibited at Vollard's three pictures which show the unmistakable influence of Lautrec, echoing the tormented emotional tension and the deft touch of the Montmartre painter. He was again in Paris in 1903, bringing with him from Barcelona some canvases whose Parisian flavour was surprising for a Spaniard, though it might be argued that his 'Jardin de Paris'

settled in Barcelona, where Don José had now been appointed art-teacher at the Barcelona Province Art School, which was known as 'La Lonja'. In Barcelona they lived first of all in the Calle Cristina, then in the Calle Llauder, and finally at No. 3 Calle de la Merced. Although the climate was less severe than at Corunna, Pablo's father now had the sensation of being in exile. For him Barcelona was a terminus, the end of a dream, the fading of all his ambitions. He no longer even attended the performances at the bull-ring to which he used to enjoy taking his son, and he was always depressed in spite of all the excitement and gaiety of Barcelona,

THE PAINTER OPISS
BARCELONA, 1897. CHARCOA

THE ARTIST'S SISTER, LOLA.
ABOUT 1896. CHARCOAL.

POSTER FOR 'ELS QUATRE GATS' (THE FOUR CATS). BARCELONA, 1902.
Foreground, Picasso: Left to right: Pere Romeu, Rocarol, Fontbona, Angel F. de Soto, Sabartés.

which meant nothing to him. "Neither Malaga, nor bulls, nor friends; just nothing at all." What else could he expect? But on the contrary, for Pablo Barcelona was a springboard from which he could set out to conquer the world. He already felt himself raised to sublime heights, for in 1896 when he was hardly fifteen, he was admitted to the Lonja *school, having completed in a single day the task set for the entrance examination, for which a month was normally allowed. Making up his mind to encourage his son to the utmost, Don José soon afterwards hired a studio in the Calle de la Plata. This was Picasso's first studio of his own. It was there that the young artist painted* Science and Charity, *a canvas for which his father worked*

dancing-girls, and women leaning against bars, show a tendency to analyse poverty and vice which he could have inherited from Ribera and Goya. In the works most directly inspired by Toulouse-Lautrec we are less conscious of the haughty pathos, the scornful elegance or bitter, sparkling irony of his master, than of Picasso's own resigned melancholy, an incurable sadness, an unchangeable sense of solitude. Picasso had painted portraits, landscapes and flower-pieces in his childhood, but now he stopped trying to paint man's outward environment and took man himself as his theme. By man, he meant Picasso himself, his own impulses and problems, his own inner conflicts, his own loves and hates. When he was twenty he saw

out both the composition and the title. This work portrays a figure on a sick-bed being attended by a doctor and a nun. Don José himself insisted on posing for the doctor, who sits in the foreground beside the bed, taking his patient's pulse. This canvas was awarded an honourable mention at the Madrid Fine Arts Exhibition in 1897.

October 1897—During the vacation there must have been much discussion in the family about Pablo's future, for at the beginning of term his Uncle Salvador's advice was followed and the boy was sent to continue his studies in Madrid. Repeating the same academic performance which had enabled him to enter the Lonja, he had himself accepted at short notice by the Royal Academy of San Fernando. But Picasso was not long in being disgusted with the official teaching and stopped attending his classes. When he fell ill at the end of the winter he decided to return to Barcelona, which he did in

THE ARTIST'S FATHER. BARCELONA, 1898.
CONTÉ, 13¼" × 9¼".

life in a gloomy and disconsolate light. But thanks to a kind of hereditary fatalism he accepted it as it was, with all its shortcomings and evils. It was only later that he was gripped by the urge to cry out in protest. Whereas most artists begin their careers in anger or revolt—witness Rouault or Ensor—but end in wisdom and serenity, Picasso gradually passed from acceptance to refusal. As he grew older he gave vent to his individualism in works of anger, revenge and loud denunciation. With years and increased experience he became only more unbridled and explosive in his protests. By the time he was world-famous and praised right and left, deluged with wealth and honours, and when he was in a position to gather in the

PICASSO AND CASAGEMAS. 1900. INDIAN INK.

June 1898, and from there went to Horta de San Juan (Horta de Ebro) together with his friend Pallarés, at whose home he was able to rest and build up his threatened health. While he was there he shared the rough, simple life of the peasants, and for him this period was in a sense an apprenticeship to existence. Long afterwards, speaking of those eight months spent in the country, he said, "I learnt everything I know in Pallarés's village."

In April 1899, on his return to Barcelona, Picasso went to live and work at the home of one of his friends at 1 Calle de los Escudilleros Blancos. The Catalan city gave him the environment his exuberant youth required. Less conservative than Madrid, Barcelona was then the centre of what amounted to an artistic renaissance. The young were received with open arms and any new idea was sure of an immediate response. Whether in the magazine Joventut *or the review*

Pel y ploma (*Fur and Feather*) *it was taken for granted that all the various currents of European thought were to be welcomed. Nietzsche and Schopenhauer, Germanic mythology and Wagner, were given the same attention as Maeterlinck, Ruskin, Verhaeren and Ibsen. In painting, Böcklin and the English pre-Raphaelites were in equal favour with the French Impressionists, news of whose works had been brought back from Paris by Ramón Casas, then a fashionable draughtsman. Miguel Utrillo was in the process of rediscovering medieval Catalan art and the painting of El Greco, while the famous 'Modern-Style' architect, Gaudi, was designing the Grüell Park. Picasso used to go to the 'Four Cats', which combined a bar with a café-concert, and which at that time was the favourite meetingplace of the young intellectuals of the city. The 'Four Cats' were none other than the founders of the establishment, an imitation of the 'Chat Noir' in Paris: these were Pere Romeu, Ramón Casas, Santiago Rusiñol and Miguel Utrillo. Here Picasso made friends with Angel and Mateo Fernandez de Soto, the poet Jaime Sabartés, the painters Carlos Casagemas, Sebastian Junyer, Nonell, Opisso, Canals, the writer Ramón Reventos, the sculptor Julio Gonzalez and many others, drawing their portraits from life as and when he happened to meet them. All these portraits were exhibited in the small*

PICASSO, SELF-PORTRAIT. MADRID, 1901.
CONTÉ. Published in *Arte Joven.*

A Vidal

— Picasso —

Paris, julio 1901

fruits of his labours, his jeers and acts of open contempt and defiance only became more frequent. His uneasy dissatisfaction has shown no signs of lessening in his old age, and he will continue serving the gods of discord and horror till the end of his days.

The *Entrance to the Bull-ring* and the *Woman with a Dog* (1900–1) were no more than works of apprenticeship. His *Self-portrait* of 1901 is more original and intimate, showing the young man staring fixedly, but with thought and resignation in his eyes, at the panorama of life. The sulky *Harlequin* leaning on a table in a café, and *The Toilet* which shows the wan figure of a woman standing in her bathtub

theatre at the 'Four Cats' some time in 1900, and not (as is often stated) in 1897. The one-man show attracted little attention, since he was just another raw Andalusian exhibiting in the café in the Calle de Montesion, and who, as yet, was hardly thought worth mentioning by the pundits.

1900—From January to September, Picasso shared a studio with his friend Casagemas in the Calle Riera de San Juan. Picasso had now thrown off any trace of academic influence and was beginning to give free rein to his own inspiration. Though he was painting, and often worked in pastel, his favourite method was still drawing; but whether he used Conté crayon, ink, charcoal or coloured chalks, everything had equal interest for him, whether street-scenes, cabarets, brothels or bull-fights. The Barcelona review Joventut *was the first journal to publish two of his drawings (12 July and 16 August 1900). At the end of October in the same year, Picasso went to Paris with Casagemas. There he found his friend,*

THE EMBRACE. BARCELONA, 1901.
CHARCOAL, $7\frac{1}{8}'' \times 5\frac{1}{8}''$.

UNG WOMAN. PARIS,
LY 1901. COLOURED CRAYON.

in the artist's poverty-stricken studio in the Boulevard de Clichy; the *Portrait of Jaime Sabartés* which reminds us of Hamlet; the *Maternity* in which, with a weary gesture, a mother is protecting her child who is already half-aware of the trials in store for him—these pictures, all of which were painted or drawn in 1901, clearly show the narrow range within which Picasso was then exploring his own sensibility. In 1902 he painted the *Women in the Bar*; they sit there, fascinated by the glass of wine that promises them only a queasy consolation and a short-lived respite. To the same period belongs the *Nude, Back-view*, from which even the faintest desire to please has been eliminated. He also painted a water-colour *Nude* which was dazzlingly precocious in its technique. But the Montmartre of the dance-halls, cabarets and impromptu singers, the Montmartre of Renoir, Lautrec and Bottini made on the whole only a superficial impression on the young Spaniard. It was rather as a worthy

the painter Nonell, who was about to leave for Barcelona and let him have his studio at 49 rue Gabrielle. He made the acquaintance of his compatriot Pere Manyac, who introduced him to Berthe Weill, the picture-dealer in the rue Victor-Massé. She bought the first canvases he ever sold in Paris, which were three bull-ring scenes, giving him 100 francs for the lot. Though Pablo went to the Louvre and the Musée du Luxembourg, he paid no less attention to what he saw in the streets, and also set himself the task of capturing the atmosphere of the Moulin de la Galette, which resulted in the most important work he produced during that stay. But as Manyac had offered him 150 francs a month for his work, Picasso decided to return to Spain that Christmas.

BIBI LA PURÉE. PARIS, 1901. CONTÉ, 18¾″ × 15⅝″. *Galerie Rosengart, Lucerne.*

THE MAN WITH THE DONKEY. PARIS, 1902.
CRAYON, 10¼″ × 7½″

Picasso
1902

WOMAN WITH A DOG. 1900–1. OIL ON CARDBOARD, 14¾″ × 16½″. *Private Collection, Paris.*

After Barcelona and Malaga, where he remained for about a fortnight, he left Casagemas and settled in Madrid in mid-January.

1901—*In Madrid, Picasso became friendly with the Catalan writer Francisco de Assis Soler, and together they undertook the founding of a review, the* Arte Joven. *The first number was ready for sale on the 31st*

of March, at 15 centimos. Soler was literary editor, while Picasso took charge of the art side. In the list of Contents such names as Unamuno, Pio Baroja, Jacinto Verdaguer and Ramón Reventos rubbed shoulders with each other. Only two or three numbers of the review managed to appear. The second number, issued on 15th April, contained portraits of the two founders

20

descendant of Valdés Leal that he expressed the mortification of the flesh in this nude—a revulsion from sensuality, rather than the intoxicating loveliness of the feminine body.

In the following year at Barcelona he came under the spell of El Greco. Now his line thinned out, his figures became elongated, the poses became more spontaneous, as can be seen in *The Old Guitar-player*, whose emaciated features, tapering into a short pointed beard, show a remarkable likeness to the portrait of *Don Rodrigo Vazquez*. The same characteristics are to be noticed in *Life*, a work in which a disillusioned symbolism brings the pleasures and sufferings of love face to face, much as in El Greco's *Sacred and Profane Love* which, however, has a religious fervour and aspiration that are entirely foreign to Picasso's temperament. Picasso was obviously trying to reassert his own manner in *The Embrace*. The brutal realism, the filling out of the volumes, the massive construction of the clasped couple and the dominant ochre of the colouring all go to show that this work has nothing in common with the Mannerism of his Blue Period. If he had prettied-up the form or warmed the colour, or if he had given the slightest touch of sensuousness to the execution, and if the two embracing figures had shared the slightest human desire instead of each remaining locked in the predestined solitude of the eternal couple, this picture would have

of the magazine, drawn by Picasso. This double portrait was accompanied by the announcement of a book they intended publishing together, to be called Madrid Art Notes (Madrid: Notas del Arte). *This never came to anything as Picasso had already left the capital.*

It is interesting to notice that this drawing was signed P. Ruiz Picasso. *Shortly afterwards Picasso stopped using anything but his mother's name for signing his work. This might seem*

surprising when we remember that Don José Ruiz was his first teacher. But as Sabartés has pointed out, "The dropping of his father's surname was not of his own choice, but depended on a particular circumstance." Not only were the artist's Catalan friends in the habit of calling him by his mother's name, but "his father's name, Ruiz, was very common, whereas the name Picasso was so unusual that it seemed ideally suited for a man whom they wanted to single out, and whose

21

been insufferable. But when we remember that the piece was painted by a young man of twenty-two, we can understand how Picasso so quickly dominated the group of artists who were then working and meeting round the Place Ravignan.

When he returned to Paris in 1904, this time to settle there, taking up his quarters in the 'Bateau-Lavoir' studio, Picasso went back to his 'Blue' manner. Then it began to develop almost systematically, if such a word may be applied to the artist's unstable temperament. This year saw the painting of the *Woman Ironing, The Actor*, and two even more characteristic works, the *Woman with the Jackdaw* and *The Two Sisters*. Picasso had seen the woman and the jackdaw at the 'Lapin Agile' cabaret run by old Frédé, whose daughter is shown stroking the bird. The emaciated, sickly face leans down over the hunched shoulders and sunken bosom. The whole composition would collapse were it not for the balance preserved by the sharp angle of the left arm. A muddy brown and diaphanous blue create an atmosphere of mystery round the ghostly form as it bends towards the cheerless bird. As for the two angular sisters whose eyes seem to be numbed by some unspoken grief, they are painted entirely in blue. What artistry is revealed, at this early stage in Picasso's development, by the freely flowing lines, the cunningly distorted forms and the planes which, under a dim light, are so

nature set him apart from all others". (Picasso, Documents iconographiques, *by Jaime Sabartés.) The fact remains that after his second trip to Paris in* 1901 *he used only his mother's name as his signature, not even keeping the initial R for Ruiz, as he had occasionally done in* 1898–99.

May 1901—*An exhibition of his work was held in the Salón Parés in Barcelona. Miguel Utrillo wrote a highly favourable article on this event,* *under the pseudonym 'Pincell' in his review* Pel y Ploma *(June number). The article was accompanied by a portrait of Picasso by Ramón Casas, showing him against an urban background portraying the Butte Montmartre, the Sacré-Cœur and the Moulin de la Galette.*

End of May—A second voyage to Paris, this time with Jaume Andreu. On his arrival Picasso went to see Manyac, who hired a studio at 130 *Boulevard de Clichy, which they*

NUDE: BACK VIEW. 1902. OIL ON CANVAS, 18⅛″ × 15⅝
Private Collection, Par

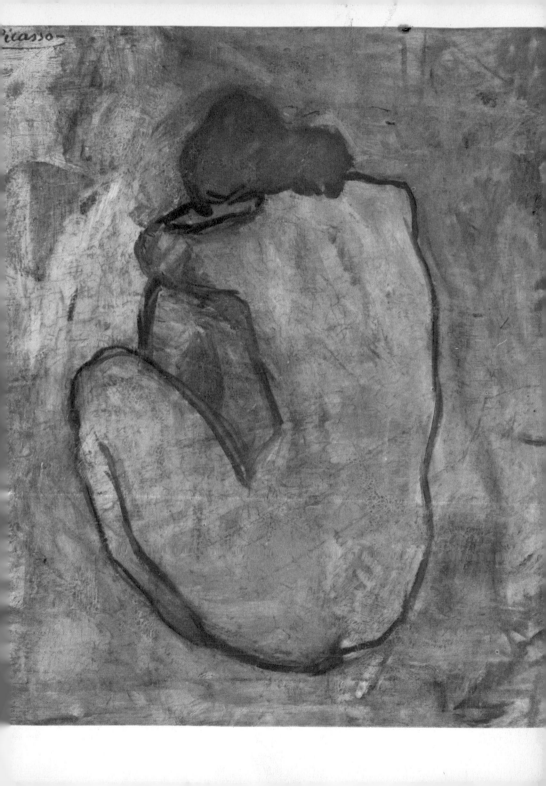

firmly related! Less analytical but drier and harsher than Toulouse-Lautrec's, his drawing is all the more dramatic as the blue tones combine to bring out its full expressiveness.

Countless reasons have been advanced in order to explain why Picasso chose the colour blue, which at that time he used more than any other. One critic says that as he was always working at night, by the dingy glimmer of a petrol-lamp, Picasso had no option but to work in monochrome. Another asserts that he was too poor to afford the tubes of colour that would be needed for enriching and enlivening his palette. Yet another suggests that the painter of *The Two Sisters* was influenced by the blue-tinted proofs which were then used by photographers instead of positive prints, which were too dear. It has also been argued that Picasso picked up this taste from his Catalan friend Nonell, whereas in actual fact the two painters were not seeing each other at the time. The exclusive use of blue is better explained by the sensual, if not spiritual, meaning of this

shared. We have a glimpse of the room they occupied in the naturalistic version of it given in The Toilet. *One of its details is important: on the wall is a poster by Toulouse-Lautrec showing the dancer May Milton, which Picasso had apparently stripped off a hoarding in Montmartre. Apart from his fellow-countrymen, Julio Gonzalez, Pablo Gargallo, Manolo and Fontbona, Picasso was without friends and lived a lonely, introspective life. He continued working under pressure, preparing the exhibition of his works which was to be held on the 24th of June 1901 at Vollard's Gallery at 6 rue Laffitte. Among the pieces he hung there, apart from the café-concert and dance-hall scenes and the pictures of races at Auteuil*

PEN AND INK, 1904.

OLD WOMAN WITH A HA
BARCELONA, 1903. PEN AND WAS

Picasso

1903

THE WOMAN WITH THE JACKDAW. PARIS, 1904. GOUACHE ON CARDBOARD, $25\frac{5}{8}'' \times 19\frac{5}{8}''$.
Toledo Museum of Art, Ohio.

and Longchamp, some attention was attracted by the landscapes, flower-pieces and reminiscences of Spain, as well as by the nudes. Most of these works were painted on cardboard. The critic Félicien Fulga spoke highly of this exhibition in La Revue Blanche. While Picasso was accused of imitating Steinlen, Lautrec, Vuillard and Van Gogh, nobody could deny the dynamic presence of a genuine painter of outstanding character. The show brought in little financial reward, but attracted the friendship of Max Jacob and the critic Gustave Coquiot, whose portraits he painted that year. Invited along to the studio by Manyac, Max Jacob spent a whole day there looking

THE TWO SISTERS. 1904. GOUACHE ON PAPER, $21\frac{5}{8}'' \times 1$
Private Collection, Pa

Picasso
1904

colour, the colour of night, ashes, melancholy and death. Bright and vivid shades would be quite inappropriate to the bloodless bodies and dark, frightened faces of human beings wilting beneath a doom they cannot understand. Cold blues and murky greys were more in keeping with that world of suffering and disinherited people.

And yet we must seek some further explanation. It is only to be found in the depths of Picasso's own character. He was already in the grip of a plastic obsession that was never to leave him. During his whole long and fertile career he has always shown the same inclination to stress volumes, combine his forms and calculate his proportions, and build up his private vision of the world on a solid linear basis, with the result that he subordinates colour to design, even at the risk of sacrificing it. This explains the large number of monochrome paintings, the austere Cubist compositions, the *Still-life with Antique Head* (1925, painted entirely in raw sienna), as well as the thinly coloured series of figures of the period 1932–35, and *Guernica* (1937), whose dramatic power is all the greater as this masterpiece is built out of nothing but contrasts of black and white. We could mention many other works to support this view, or we could draw attention to the engravings and sculptures in which he concentrated all his powers as a draughtsman and plastic artist. "I have no idea whether I'm a great painter," he said to Max Jacob,

through piles of pictures. It was the beginning of a long friendship between the poet and the painter.

When at the end of autumn 1901 Jaime Sabartés rejoined Picasso in Paris, he was dumbfounded by the deep and unforeseen changes that had taken place in his friend's painting as he was entering on his Blue Period. The gaily coloured street-scenes and spectacular portraits of a few months earlier had been replaced by strange personalities in the grip of sorrow or

hunger, and most frequently set against an unrelieved blue background. It was during that particularly gloomy winter that Picasso worked on the famous portrait of Jaime Sabartés which is now in the Museum of Western Art in Moscow, and which is sometimes known as The Bock. *At the end of December Picasso left Paris for Barcelona, which meant that the informal contract binding him to Manyac lapsed. The truth is that they both welcomed the break. For Manyac it was a*

29

"but I am a great draughtsman." In spite of some perfect successes in which the colour is cleverly or generously exploited, Picasso has been at his most expressive in works in which the colour is toned down or impoverished and even mortified: then he really achieves greatness.

If we compare *The Two Sisters* or the *Woman with the Jackdaw* with *The Embrace*, we can see exactly how the artist's style had changed. Less modelled but more graphic, less eloquent but more solid and showing more regard for surfaces, yet at the same time more mysterious and more emotional, it emanates a profound human sympathy. In the same year Picasso entered a new phase of his evolution. There was not a hint of blue in his *Clown on Horseback* (1905), while in the family of *Tumblers* (1905) pink is the dominant colour; this becomes even more marked in *The Athlete*, *Riding Horses to Water*, *Nude Drawing back her Hair*, and the *Tall Pink Nude* (1905). His harlequins, columbines and acrobats have still the same under-fed and gloomy appearance. But they are no longer ragged outcasts with empty bellies and hearts heavy with despair: wanderers still, they are grave rather than grief-stricken, timid rather than wistful, people who are sustained by their own dreams, rather than crushed by their destiny. They are no longer imprisoned in some unbearable loneliness, but they live now in families or teams, with the men,

financial relief, since his protégé's new manner did not appeal to collectors, while for Picasso it was a matter of regaining his liberty.

1902—He remained in Barcelona from January to October. He was then living with his parents, Calle de la Merced, while working in a room in the Calle Conde del Asalto which he shared as a studio with the painter Rocarol, and which at the same time served as Angel F. de Soto's lodgings. As if to outwit the misery and penury

they had to put up with, he painted on the walls of this room all the essential —and even luxurious—items of furniture which the three friends were unable to buy. It was a time of want and anguish. The bleak melancholy which had invaded Picasso's work was like some inner burden he carried wherever he went. He had just turned twenty and believed, like many of his Catalan friends, that "Art is the child of sorrow and pain". In his absence Manyac organized an exhibition in

TH WEARING A FRILLED COLLAR. PARIS, 1905.
ACHE ON CARDBOARD, 31¼″ × 23⅜″.
anonymous loan to Worcester Art Museum (U.S.A.).

women, children and tamed or domestic animals all sharing the same conditions. In grouping them the artist had to strive after unity of composition, and to portray them properly he had to situate them in space. As a result there were no more drab backgrounds from now on, no vague limbo or rarefied atmosphere making for baffled thought and anaemic form. Becoming less disjointed and caricatural, the drawing takes on a classical fullness. If a certain amount of blue still lingers in the works of the Pink Period, it is only there to carry out its proper function, on the same terms as red, brown, green or yellow.

The *Acrobats with a Dog* look as if they have just left their trapeze and landed in the middle of some twilight landscape. The family of *Tumblers* or Jugglers seem to have come to a stop in the open fields, in the interval between two engagements in their foot-loose odyssey. The *Family of Acrobats* is sitting on the outskirts of a wood: this water-colour has a gentleness, grace and tenderness of quality not often found in Picasso's work. It is a kind of 'Holy Family' as seen by some twentieth-century Raphael. It has delicacy of touch, there is originality in the diagonal composition, and there is throughout

Paris, at Berthe Weill's, with the canvases he had left behind. This was held from 1st to 15th April, and was sponsored by Adrien Farge. Although this took place at the height of his Blue Period, none of Picasso's most recent works were shown: the exhibits all dated from his last stay in Paris, and for the most part were painted before the beginning of winter 1901. October 1902—*Picasso now returned to Paris and this time set up studio on the Left Bank at the Hôtel des Écoles, rue Champollion. His friend Sebastian Junyer accompanied him on this third trip. During the six*

BRONZE HEAD. 1906. Height, 4¾".

NUDE. BARCELONA, 1902
WATER-COLOUR, 10⅝″ × 7⅞″
Private Collection, Paris

Picasso

a lightness and subtlety of tone. In the *Harlequin's Family* the man is holding a child in his arms and watching his wife at her toilet. It is an intimate scene, full of peace and trust, without a trace of the sadness, bitterness or tragedy of the traditional clown. Their tent is at rest during one of the intervals in their endless wandering. There is both dignity and familiarity in the poses, an elegant soberness in the drawing, and the colouring is full of harmony. Where there is a contrast, as between the red tunic and the bluish ground of the *Youth Wearing a Frilled Collar*, the artist carefully tones it down by a gradation of greys, so as to avoid spoiling the subdued radiance of the adolescent profile—a profile, by the way, which is almost a replica of that of the *Woman with the Fan*. It is interesting to note, in the works of that short period, how slight was the distinction he made between the sexes. With their equally effeminate features, multicoloured or checked tights and loose, floating dresses, both the men and the women seem to have stepped from the same world of fantasy and dream. The same ambiguity is to be found in the studies of nudes: for instance, in the undeveloped *Girl with a Basket of Flowers*, with her narrow hips and little breasts, and in the *Tall Pink Nude*, where the artist has given his female model a distinctly masculine body. We do not know what can have prompted this extraordinary series of works. Had Picasso been looking too intently

months of this stay he changed his lodgings three times: after the Hôtel des Ecoles he went to the Hôtel du Maroc (now Hôtel Louis XV) in the rue de Seine; here he rented a miserable attic where he was not even alone, since he had to share the place with a sculptor called Sisket. Not long afterwards Max Jacob, who was then working in business, offered him a share in a room he had recently taken on the Boulevard Voltaire. Picasso moved in at once, delighted to rejoin his friend. Life was

neither easy nor gay, however. Picasso used to work all night, while in the daytime Max Jacob had to go to his office and it was Picasso's turn to get some sleep. However, they found great and genuine consolation in reading poetry together. Tiring at last of Paris, Picasso again thought of returning to Barcelona, where at least he would feel more at home. In order to pay for his railway-ticket he did his best to sell a few canvases and was prepared to accept as little as 200 francs for them

WOMAN WITH THE FAN. PARIS, 1905. OIL, 39⅜″ ×
Mrs. W. Averell Harriman Collection, New

at the frescoes of Puvis de Chavannes, or the decadent day-dreams of Sérusier, or the somewhat precious pastels of Odilon Redon? It is true that he was not unaware of Cézanne, as there is an obvious affinity between Picasso's *Naked Boy Leading a Horse* and *The Bather* in the Lecomte collection.

At all events the influences then at work on Picasso helped to free him from the inner complexes and the morbid realism of the Blue Period. His pink manner shows a much reduced tension which he was able to exploit to the full. It allowed him to find new subject-matter, to shake off his morbid tendencies, to perfect his drawing which now became more purely linear, and, though this is almost impossible to define, somehow to integrate his forms more satisfactorily into the structure of the composition. Picasso could not long remain faithful to a style which was so little suited to his own temperament, with its scarcely modelled figures, its limpid, diffuse light, its dim reds, washed-out blues and shabby whites, a world that seemed to have neither weight nor structure nor movement, where all was transient, unreal, mannered and sickly. He now engraved the sixteen etchings of the series of *Acrobats* (Saltim-banques) which Vollard later published in 1913. In 1906 he painted *The Coiffure, The Woman with a Loaf of Bread,* and *The Toilet.* In the last-named piece we observe the contrast between the graceful pose

all. But the collectors held back and he could not even find a gallery to look after them in his absence. When everything else failed he went across to Montmartre and left his works in the keeping of his friend Pichot. When at last he succeeded in selling one of his pastels to a Madame Bernard for 60 francs, he made up his mind to go back to Spain. It was so cold at the time, that in order to keep warm the day before he left he burnt an enormous number of drawings and water-colours

which had accumulated during the year, both in Barcelona and Paris. The water-colour reproduced on page 33, made at Barcelona early in 1902, is one of the very few specimens of his work to have survived from that time. Early 1903—Picasso found himself back in Barcelona, where in the Calle Riera de San Juan he and Angel F. de Soto shared a studio which he had already occupied with Casagemas in 1900. This coming year was to be one of the most fruitful periods of his

RIDING HORSES TO WATER. GOUACHE ON CARDBOARD, $14\frac{3}{4}'' \times 22\frac{7}{8}''$. *On anonymous loan to the Worcester Art Museum, U.S*

youth, with freshly painted canvases piling up as though he were haunted by some obsession that he was trying to shake off. He now painted The Old Jew, Célestine, *the* Soler Family's Picnic, *the* Old Guitar-player, The Poor Folk at the Sea-side, The Embrace, *and finally the allegorical piece,* Life. *At the same time he was busy on a series of portraits, including those of Angel F. de Soto, Corina Romeu, and early in 1904, Jaime Sabartés. He was no longer interested in anything but human beings, and*

there is no trace of any still-life in his output at that time.

April 1904—Picasso returned to Paris for the fourth time, and was to settle there finally. As on the previous occasion he was accompanied by Sebastian Junyer. One of his compatriots, the sculptor Paco Durio, let him have his studio, so he moved into the 'Bateau-Lavoir' at 13 rue Ravignan, now the Place Émile Godeau. He remained there until October 1909. The five years spent by Picasso in that humble studio were to prove decisive.

38

THE HARLEQUIN'S FAM
PARIS, 1905. GOUACHE, $22\frac{7}{8}'' \times$
Lewisohn Collection, New Y

Picasso
1905

of the naked woman and the extreme stylization of the servant with the mirror: there is a similar contrast between the softly pink-tinted flesh and the blue dress of the *Woman with the Loaf of Bread*. There were signs of some return to the humanitarianism of the Blue Period in the *Acrobat Sitting with a Child*, before renewing his inspiration by contact with pre-romantic Iberian sculpture. The *Self-Portrait* of 1906 is full of significance in this respect. Shortly afterwards Gauguin's primitivism seems to have attracted him for a while.

Whatever else he was doing, the Pink Period was now at an end. He had already sensed its dangers in 1905, and his reaction was to turn with enthusiasm to a form of art he had first approached in 1899, namely sculpture. The *Bronze Harlequin* of 1905 shows how difficult it must have been to escape from the influence of Rodin. But the *Head* of 1906 shows signs of a fresh line of approach which

For the moment—we are still in 1905 —his work showed some slackening of tension. The blind beggars and grieving women of the Blue Period now gave way to a world of harlequins, acrobats and strolling players. The pink is blended with blue in order to soften its austerity, and to bring out gracefulness. But can it be said that at the time when this transformation was taking place, Picasso's private life was undergoing some profound change? There is no evidence of this. No doubt his association with circus-people gave him the models for his canvases, but the transformation that was going on was also part of a kind of research in which anecdote had only a minor part to play. The changing choice of subjects shows entirely new plastic theories at work, rather than any marked change on the moral plane.

STUDY FOR 'THE BOY WITH A PIPE'. PARIS, 1905.
PEN AND INK, 11¾″ × 9″. *Cone Collection, Museum of Art, Baltimore.*

STUDY FOR 'THE HAREM'. 1905. CONTÉ, $22\frac{5}{8}'' \times 18\frac{1}{8}''$.

was directly opposed to Rodin's impressionism. This work, which is of great importance though it is small, shows an effort towards synthesis and density that marks Picasso's break with the naturalist technique of illusionism. From now on all his faculties were to be applied to the fundamental problem of volume. After appearing fairly indifferent to plastic form during the preceding five years, in 1906 he began to show an interest in form that has never slackened since. The statues, pictures and drawings that came from his hands were all dictated by what might be called strictly sculptural requirements. The *Woman's Head in Red* of 1907, the effigies he carved in wood as well as the bronze mask of the same year, all have a 'primitive' quality which the artist probably took from Gauguin rather than from African carvings, though the period beginning in 1907 has sometimes been called his 'Negro' period. Is it true that it was Matisse who initiated Picasso into African art? The two painters became friends in 1906. Matisse is said to have discovered, at Père Sauvage's shop in the rue de Rennes, a carving from the Ivory Coast which he showed to his friend. But Picasso has always maintained that he was not influenced by African art before 1910. It is none the less disturbing to notice that the right-hand section of the *Young Ladies of Avignon*, in which some critics detect a foretaste of Cubism, as well as several 'studies' done in that period and

The Bateau-Lavoir, which from then onwards became a sort of shrine of national importance, is a strange, rickety, noisy building made up of a haphazard combination of beams and planks, and full of dark and unexpected corners. Built half-way up the Butte Montmartre, overlooking little gardens on one side (for at that time the Butte was in the outskirts of the city) and on the other side facing towards the old fortifications, the Bateau-Lavoir was a kind of maze

for the unwary visitor. The studio occupied by Picasso, like all the rest, was extremely poor: there was no furniture to speak of, only a mattress (a divan without legs), a whitewood table, a rusty old iron stove, a chair and a black trunk for people to sit on. In those days Pablo wore only the blue overall and pullover which plumbers then used for their work. His life was worse than hard, for even necessities were beyond his purse. Clients were few and the artists, who felt themselves

43

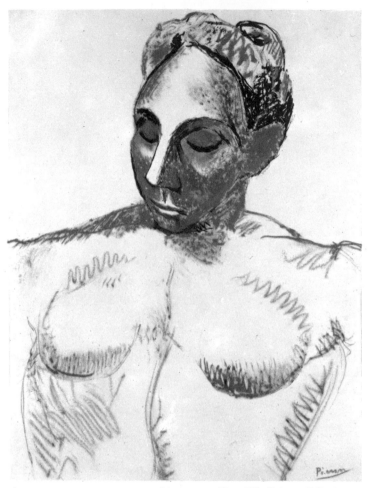

WOMAN'S HEAD IN RED. WINTER 1906–7. OIL, $25\frac{5}{8}'' \times 18\frac{1}{2}''$. *Private Collection, Paris.*

to be outcasts in an indifferent and selfish society (those were the 'Good old days' of the Edwardians!) had nothing to sustain them but a belief in their own genius. The rue Laffitte dealers, Clovis Sagot and Ambroise Vollard certainly bought a canvas from time to time, but that was not enough

to live on. On days of absolute famine the artists went along to old Père Soulier, who had a junk-shop in the rue des Martyrs and who gave cash for whatever was offered him.

Picasso widened his circle of friends while living at the Bateau-Lavoir. Apart from the nucleus of Spaniards

44

WOMAN'S HEAD. PARIS, 1905–6. CHARCOAL, 24⅝″ × 18¾″.

living in Paris, with whom he never lost touch, he was friendly with his neighbour Van Dongen, as well as Maurice Raynal, Alfred Jarry, André Salmon, Pierre MacOrlan and, later on, Pierre Reverdy. His faithful friend Max Jacob shared not only the day-to-day troubles but the occasional feasts as well. The picture would be incomplete without Guillaume Apollinaire, whom he met in 1905 and who at once published an enthusiastic article about him in La Plume (16th May); then there was Matisse whom he met in 1906 at Gertrude Stein's; Juan Gris, Derain, Georges Braque,

45

notably the *Head* which is reproduced on page 59 and resembles an African mask, all show some relationship to the pieces of carving brought over from Africa by colonials. In any case the *Young Ladies of Avignon* shows more decidedly constructivist tendencies than the *Portrait of Gertrude Stein* or the *Self-Portrait* of 1906. But before tracing Picasso's struggle towards creating a new vision and a new inventory of the external world, there are a few other important questions to be answered.

Here we have a young Spaniard settling in France, in search of a suitable climate for his creative powers to develop. It was of his own accord that he sought to make contact with French art, and in particular French Impressionism, the supremacy of which was no longer challenged even by the general public, that same public which only twenty years before had greeted the new aesthetic with scathing sarcasm. Why did this Spaniard, so sensitive to the various trends of his century and so receptive to every influence, never once try to follow up the experiments of Renoir, Monet or Pissarro? If that line seemed to him to be already worked out or discredited, why then did he not fall in with his friends Matisse and Braque? Why did he refuse to subscribe to Fauvism, a movement which was then rallying so many determined young painters who had washed their hands of the old tradition and were longing for something entirely new? For

whose acquaintance he made through Apollinaire in 1907, and finally Kahnweiler, who supported him from 1907 onwards and became his dealer. Thus a whole group of painters gradually clustered round the Bateau-Lavoir, as well as poets and critics, whose combined onslaught was soon to rock the traditional foundations of painting and of art as a whole. It was during the unusually eventful year 1905 that Picasso met Fernande Olivier. Meeting her at the fountain where the

Bateau-Lavoir residents went to draw water, he asked her to come and see his paintings, and these no doubt appealed to the beautiful young woman, since they decided to share the hardships and joys of life together.
Summer 1905—At the invitation of his friend the Dutch columnist Tom Schilperoot, Picasso went to Holland for a month. He cannot have found that misty, melancholy land very inspiring, but if only through the relaxation it gave him, this journey seems to

THE ATHLETE. 1905. GOUACHE ON CARDBOARD, 21¼″ × 17⅜″. *Private Collection, Paris.*

have strengthened his resolve to return to a more objective view of the world. In such works as the Woman with the Fan *and* The Youth Wearing a Frilled Collar, *he was able to establish a sort of balance between the human and the traditional which only a period of happiness and repose could*

it must not be forgotten that nobody was ever more observant than Picasso, more attentive to the discoveries of his age, more prompt to receive and absorb its many innovations, no matter where they came from. This independent but always open-minded man, for ever on the alert and quick to seize on whatever he could make use of, passed by the respected masters of the French school without as much as a glance in their direction. He lived among the *avant-garde* of contemporary painters without feeling the slightest urge to follow them, and was completely unmoved by the birth and growth of Fauvism.

His attitude can easily be defended, though not on racial grounds, since Zuloaga was also a Spaniard and had adhered to the Impressionist programme; and not just by his contrariness, since the best way of destroying the remnants of Impressionism was surely by joining the Fauves. The truth is that as soon as he grew conscious of his own vocation, and for the rest of his career, Pablo Picasso remained first and foremost an individualist, fascinated by the plastic values of things, their structure and their relief, and by a sculptural

give. Picasso here seems to have achieved a degree of perfection beyond which it would be hard to avoid falling into Mannerism. In other words, was he to content himself, like other artists, with always painting the same picture over and over again? It was in this dilemma that Picasso once more turned to sculpture (see page 32), obviously in the hope of rediscovering, by this round-about means, a new sense of volume and fullness of form. Thus everything he did during 1906 was directed towards this new objective, which involved replacing the values of the harlequins of the Pink Period, which he thought were too sentimental, by purely plastic considerations. The time he spent at Gosol, a little town

WOMAN'S HEAD, PROFILE. PARIS, 1905.
DRY-POINT, $11\frac{1}{2}'' \times 9\frac{7}{8}''$.

Picasso
1905

SALOME. PARIS, 1905. DRY-POINT, $15\frac{3}{4}'' \times 13\frac{5}{8}''$.

in Lerida province in Spain, during the summer of 1906 *in the company of Fernande Olivier, helped to quicken this evolution. Such works as* The Toilet, *the* Portrait of Fernande, *the* Woman with the Loaf of Bread *show a certain stiffening of posture and a simplification of the*

volumes, which relates them more closely to the Portrait of Gertrude Stein *and the* Two Enlaced Nudes, *both dating from late* 1906, *than to the harlequins of the year before. At the same time the colour was modified and given more body, moving from the pink shades into the duller range of ochres.*

49

YOUNG MAN'S HEAD. PARIS, 1906. OIL.   *Private Collection, Paris.*

The Portrait of Gertrude Stein has a story attached to it. The American writer Gertrude Stein settled in France in 1904 with her brother Leo, and became one of Picasso's first admirers. She knew nothing of the artist's work when she *bought* The Girl with the Basket of Flowers *for 150 francs at Clovis Sagot's in the rue Laffitte. Eager to know the artist who painted it, she called at the Bateau-Lavoir, and on her first visit bought 800 francs worth of pictures. This woman's fearless*

TOILET. GOSOL, SUMMER 1906. OIL, $58\frac{1}{4}'' \times 38\frac{5}{8}''$.
right Art Gallery, Buffalo (N.Y.).

Picas
17

THE ACROBATS. PARIS, 1905. DRY-POINT, $11\frac{3}{8}'' \times 12\frac{7}{8}''$.

gaze, her poise, her determined expression, her broad, mannish shoulders, appealed to Picasso, and he suggested painting her portrait. Gertrude Stein at once agreed. The first sittings were held during the winter of 1905–6. The American has told how "Picasso sat very tight in his chair and very close to his canvas and on a very small palette which was of a uniform brown-grey colour began mixing some more brown-grey." This sitting was fol-

lowed by about ninety more. Despairing of ever finishing the portrait, for he was not satisfied with the face, one day Picasso blocked out the entire head. "When I look at you I stop seeing you," he said impatiently to Gertrude Stein. So the portrait remained half-painted. It was only some months later, on his return from Gosol, that he took up the canvas and finished it in the absence of the model.

But Picasso's restlessness was already

seeking other outlets. At the end of 1906, *with a view to an important composition,* The Young Ladies of Avignon, *he began a series of studies which set him far more difficult problems than those he had so far been solving.*

We are now on the eve of the Cubist adventure, when Picasso was only twenty-five years of age. The general public did not even know his name and yet he already had a considerable output behind him. A tireless draughtsman, he could count his drawings by hundreds: he could handle pencil, charcoal, coloured crayon, the pen, and indian ink with equal fluency. As an engraver he had already produced etchings of an irreproachable classicism, and had already used drypoint, and carved woodcuts. On two occasions, in 1899 and 1905–6 he had proved himself a skilled and enterprising sculptor. He had also painted more than two hundred pictures in watercolour, gouache, pastel and oil. His output was already enormous and spread over a wide range. He had tried all the various mediums and genres with the same ease and the same agility of mind, excelling alike in portraiture and composition, still-life and landscape. All this he did without the least hint of repetition and without the slightest fatigue, for it is quite true that "whatever he attempted, the first sketch and the finished canvas were equally attractive" (A. Level). Success was now within sight. Picasso had no illusions; he knew that the time

WOMAN AT THE MARKET. 1906. *Museum of Art, Baltimore.*

53

THE YOUNG LADIES OF AVIGNON. PARIS, SPRING 1907. OIL, $96\frac{1}{2}'' \times 92\frac{1}{2}''$. *Museum of Modern Art, New York*

expression of forms. The transient flux of Impressionist painting could not appeal to him, any more than the tendency towards decoration, the flat, raw colours and often slipshod drawing of the Fauves. In any case he was much too intellectual an artist to be satisfied with pure sensation. If he took no part in the researches of the sensualists and hedonists, except for his own amusement or as an act of defiance, and if he never practised decorative art or the lavish display of colour for their own sake, on the other hand he was always extremely attentive to all the efforts going on around him so long as they concerned form, space and composition. When Cubism was still at the lisping stage in the Montparnasse studios, he took it over and gave it depth and proclaimed its laws, imposing it first on Montmartre and then on the rest of the world. When he was a prey to uncertainties and doubts, the masters to whom he turned for instruction or consolation were Ingres, Cézanne, Courbet and other structuralists or architects of painting who were the zealous advocates of form. Far more than the arts of the East, with their serene harmonies and luxurious polychromes which, however, lack weight, modelling and depth, it was the archaic or primitive arts which struck a cord in him, Iberian sculpture, Negro carving or pre-Columbian ceramics, but always only the formal, three-dimensional arts.

had come to listen to the inner daemon which was to carry him from victory to victory. Yielding to the tyrannical need for absolute creation, which meant that every one of his works had to be at once a problem set and a problem solved, he took it on himself to break the spell that threatened to frustrate him, and to adventure alone up the steep path leading to knowledge. This meant choosing the lot of the revolutionary. It was a painful undertaking, which demanded such an effort of the imagination that a great deal of trial and error was inevitable. For instance, there are at least seventeen sketches or drafts for the composition of the Young Ladies of Avignon. In addition Picasso had to make countless drawings for the various figures, and it is interesting to note that most of these studies date from the end of 1906 and that many others were made even after the picture was finished or at any rate discarded. The first version contained seven figures—five female

His 'Pink Period' had freed him from the expressionistic realism of the 'Blue Period'. To the delicate Pink Period mannerism there now succeeded the robust lyricism of the Negro Period. The *Two Enlaced Nudes* of 1906 is already remarkable for the powerful structure of the figures, their massive limbs, the striking contrast between the different planes, the strange incurvation of the nose which heralds the mask-like faces of the *Avignon Dancer* or the *Young Ladies of Avignon* of 1907, or of the *Woman with White Linen* (1907). Was this, then, his 'Negro Period'? Since Picasso always denied that he was influenced by Negro art, it must have been from primitive Iberian sources and the exoticism of Gauguin's woodcarvings that he took these simplified figures and the bold distortions and geometrical presentation of these works. The *Young Ladies of Avignon*, that great canvas which has been so frequently described and interpreted, is of prime importance in the sense of being the concrete outcome of an original vision, and because it points to a radical change in the aesthetic basis as well as the technical processes of painting. In itself the work does not bear very close scrutiny, for the drawing is hasty and the colour unpleasant, while the composition as a whole is confused and there is too much concern for effect and far too much gesticulation in the figures. Was this how Picasso invented Cubism? A few sharp angles, a few brutal ellipses, the violent twist in the

nudes and two men. One of the men, seated in the centre, was the figure of a sailor of whom Picasso made two particularly thorough paintings, one of them with him smoking a cigarette. On the left was a student entering the room with a skull in his hand. In the second version the sailor was replaced by a female nude, but there were still seven figures. It was only in the third version that two of the women, originally placed to the left of the picture, were dropped out, while the student

with the skull was replaced by a woman drawing a curtain and occupying a position very like that which is shown in the final version. The title of the picture was not supplied by the artist, but it was André Salmon, apparently, who gave it this name years after it was completed. When Picasso started work on it early in 1907, he and his friends used to call it, more crudely, 'The Avignon brothel', in ironic reference to a certain house in the Calle d'Avignon in Barcelona. The title was no more than a studio joke, and if it did not exactly justify the sailor's presence in the first version, at least it helps to explain it; whereas the current title has no meaning whatever, the work having been completely transformed under the artist's hand. The Young Ladies of Avignon *canvas has had a curious history. Like some laboratory experiment, for a long time it was known only to the artists and connoisseurs who saw it in the rue de Ravignan studio. Everything goes to prove that it shocked by its novelty. Kahnweiler, who had just opened a gallery at 28 rue Vignon, has recorded the surprising terms in which Wilhelm Uhde, who already knew Picasso, described it to him: he said there was "something Assyrian about it". This was enough to shake even the least prejudiced of Picasso's circle. Kahnweiler at once went over to the Bateau-Lavoir and everything suggests that his astonishment gave way to admiration, since by the following year he was Picasso's exclusive dealer and a very firm friend. Incidentally, we might now recall that although certain connoisseurs of painting, such as Gertrude Stein, Wilhelm Uhde, R. Dutilleul, H. Rupf, Stchoukine and V. Kramar stood by Picasso when he began his adventure into the dangerous experiment of Cubism, quite a number then stopped buying his canvases, while even his first patron Ambroise Vollard refused to commit himself for some time.*

NUDE. PARIS, 1907. WASH, $11\frac{3}{4}'' \times 7\frac{1}{2}''$.

When Georges Braque himself first saw the Young Ladies of Avignon *at the end of spring 1907, no argument or reasoning could convert him to it: his view was that to paint in such a way was as bad as drinking petrol in the hope of spitting fire. None the less, his own experience in the course of the winter of 1907–8 was to lead him to*

57

features of the two right-hand figures—was this all that was required in order to proclaim the canons of the modern plastic arts? Conventional curves, blank surfaces and flat stretches of colour still predominate. The truth is that this famous canvas was significant for what it anticipated rather than for what it achieved: the end of naturalism and imitation, a passionate quest for an art stripped of the old make-believe and moribund rules, an art dictated by the imagination and returning to its origins. Obviously, with its frankness of execution, its disturbing emphasis, its savage stylization, the *Young Ladies of Avignon* was far removed from the severe discipline, the analytical style and strict logic that were to characterize the painting of both Picasso and Braque in 1909. Picasso was not advancing along this new road entirely alone. Was it, then, he who prepared the way? In other words, was he really the inventor of Cubism?

Albert Gleizes has loudly claimed this distinction for himself and his group of friends. Gleizes has asserted that Cubism emerged from the efforts of the little group consisting of Metzinger, Léger, Le Fauconnier and himself. They were working in Montparnasse and shared an intense admiration for Cézanne, while knowing nothing whatever of the experiments of Picasso, Juan Gris, Gargallo, Marcoussis, Severini and the other French or foreign artists who were then living in Montmartre, until the time when either Guillaume

solutions that were not so remote from those which Picasso had just discovered.

Finally, it is also surprising that this now universally known canvas was only reproduced for the first time in 1925, in the 15th July number of The Surrealist Revolution *and was hung for the first time in the Petit Palais in 1937, during the Paris International Exhibition.*

During 1908 Cézanne, an important retrospective exhibition of whose works *had been shown the year before in the autumn Salon, was the order of the day in the Montmartre as well as in the Montparnasse studios. Picasso remained even less immune than the others from this tyrannical influence. On the contrary, he seems to have welcomed it as a discipline through which he could strengthen himself before exploring further. It was in this state of mind that he worked on a series of landscapes in the summer, while 'relaxing' at La-Rue-des-Bois,*

HEAD. PARIS, 1907. OIL.   *Private Collection, Paris.*

a little village 4 kilometres outside Creil, in the Oise (see the Cottage in a Garden). *During the same summer Braque painted, at L'Estaque (Marseilles), the landscapes which were rejected by the autumn Salon* and then shown from 9th–28th November at Kahnweiler's gallery, and which gave the critic Louis de Vauxcelles the opportunity of distinguishing himself yet again by inventing the term Cubism, just as in

STUDY FOR 'FRIENDSHIP'. 1908. PEN AND INK, 19″ × 12⅜″.

1905 *he had given their name to the* 'Fauves'. *Perhaps it was one word too many, but it was to be an enormous success.*

But already Picasso was beginning to turn his attention elsewhere: what interested him now was the expression of the human figure by exclusively plastic means. Radically reducing the body of his Seated Nude and his

Apollinaire or Max Jacob took the initiative of bringing the two groups together. According to Gleizes it was in the course of that memorable meeting that Picasso picked out from the work of the Montparnasse group those explosive elements which his genius turned into a revolution. Whatever the truth of this, in any case 1908 was a most crucial year for painting, in which these two groups came together and vied in their admiration for Cézanne. Cézanne had been the first to proclaim that everything in nature is made up of cylinders, cones and spheres. He was thus the 'father' of the greatest plastic revolution ever attempted since Paolo Uccello.

"When we invented Cubism", Picasso has said, "we had no idea that we were creating it, but we were only trying to express what we felt inside us." An instinctive desire for a better architectural basis and a complete knowledge of the object in itself was generally shared by all the best painters of that time. From 1908 both Picasso and Braque were trying to represent volume by drawing alone, the latter starting from nature, whereas Picasso was trying to re-create it in his own mind. Impressionism was dead. The century that had

Nude in the Forest (1908)—*both of which are in the Moscow Museum of Modern Art—to a monochrome equation, he was asserting his sculptural bent, as though seeking through this medium to check the correctness of his analysis. At one bound Cézanne was left far behind. Later, while discussing these works with his friend the sculptor, Julio Gonzalez, Picasso himself pointed out that it would suffice to cut up these paintings—in which the colours were no more than indications of perspectives, or planes inclining this way and that—and to reassemble them according to the instructions given by the colours*

COMPOSITION. 1909.
CONTÉ, 12″ × 12″.

HOUSES ON A HILL-SIDE. HORTA DE EBRO, SUMMER 1909. OIL, $36\frac{1}{4}'' \times 25\frac{5}{8}''$. *Private Collection, Paris.*

themselves, in order to find oneself looking at pieces of sculpture. The painting would be equal to this test. We cannot leave the year 1908 without mentioning the banquet which was organized by the artists of the Bateau-Lavoir in honour of Douanier Rousseau. It was Picasso who took the initiative and the dinner was held in his studio. To make ready for the ceremony, the walls were stripped of their usual decorations. All that was left, in prominent places, were a few beautiful Negro masks, while the place of honour was filled by the por-

trait of Yedwiga, *painted by Rousseau and which Picasso had recently bought from old Soulier. At the far end of the room stood the improvised 'throne' on which the Douanier was to sit in state. The guests were significant: the representatives of 'Art' were Georges Braque, Jacques Vaillant and Agéro; the writers were Apollinaire, Max Jacob, André Salmon, Maurice Cremnitz, René Dalize and Gertrude Stein. In every respect the ceremony was an essentially Montmartre event. If the cooking was rather casual, there was no lack of wine. They*

AMBROISE VOLLARD. PARIS, 1910. OIL, $36\frac{1}{4}'' \times 25\frac{5}{8}''$.
Modern Art Museum, Moscow

just sown its wild oats with Fauvism seemed already to be repenting of its haste. The painter withdrew behind closed doors and started thinking for himself. In the privacy of his studio he took stock of the familiar things round about him, the decanter and wine-glass, the packet of tobacco, the guitar. He observed them from different angles, he felt them over and over again with his expert fingers, he looked through them, so to speak, with the astonished vision of his own senses; he studied their inner movement, their secret mechanism, he steeped himself in their immanence, their presence. In his solitude he relived the genesis of all things, he felt in his own being the renewed creation of the world. Nothing evaded his grasp, for he found his way to the centre of things by virtue of a power that was neither pride nor love, but consent and respect. The object then appeared to him in its total form, with its armature, its outlines and contours, its inner structure, its underneath: when he was able to show it as it was, then Cubism was born. That is what Picasso did. That is how he rediscovered the hidden springs which bind man to

had also invited a pompous individual with a white beard, a restorer of old paintings who lived in the house and who was introduced to the Douanier as 'The Minister of Fine-Arts'. On the table-top, Apollinaire improvised a long poem singing the praises of Rousseau, in which fact and fiction were wonderfully mixed. Then came a series of speeches to which the worthy Douanier, who had thought- fully brought his violin with him, replied by playing some tunes of his own composition, including 'The Little Bells' and a waltz called 'Clemency'. A number of quite his- torical pronouncements were made that evening, thanks no doubt to the alcohol: for instance, Rousseau, delighted by

HEAD. PARIS, 1909.
WATER-COLOUR, $24\frac{5}{8}'' \times 18\frac{1}{2}''$.

reality, at once possessing and possessed, containing in himself all the elements of the universe, just as the universe contains him. It is thus that he found out how to convey a sensation of volume on a flat surface, without depending any longer on linear perspective, fore-shortening, modelling, chiaroscuro or all the bag of tricks that had been used by the museum-painters down the centuries. From Horta de Ebro, where he spent the summer, he returned with the *Houses on the Hillside* and *Fernande* (1909)—a landscape and portrait in which he passed beyond what Cézanne had to teach and laid down the rudiments of a new language. In Paris he painted a series of still-lifes, the *Portrait of Braque*, the *Woman in Green*, and also sculpted a *Woman's Head* according to the same principles. In these various pictures we find a new conception of space in which the planes are geometrically defined instead of being plotted according to the vanishing-lines of the classical canon, and start from the canvas to focus in the eye of the spectator. In 1910 he went on to produce his famous series, *The Girl with the Mandoline* the portraits of *Vollard*,

his reception, whispered confidentially into Picasso's ear, "After all, you and I are both great painters: myself in the Modern style, and you in the Egyptian."

1909-13—Heroic years, indeed, during which the only satisfactory chronology to follow is that of the works themselves, so closely had the artist's life become bound up with the experiment on which he had launched himself body and soul. His development may thus be shown without recourse to anecdote. If we mention the various periods that Picasso spent each summer at Horta de San Juan, Cadaqués, Céret or Sorgues during these four years, it is because these names offer useful points of reference for plotting

WOMAN'S HEAD. 1909.
BRONZE. HEIGHT, 16½".

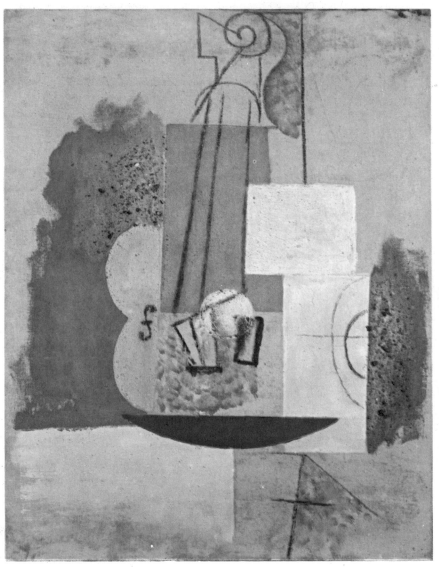

VIOLIN. PARIS, WINTER 1912. OIL AND SAND, 18⅛″ × 15″.   *Private Collection, Paris.*

Kahnweiler and *Wilhelm Uhde*, and the *Nude* painted during a holiday at Cadaqués, where he stayed with Derain. The following summer he went to Céret with Braque, and brought back with him *The Accordion-player* and *The Man with the Pipe* (1911). We have only to compare these two canvases with those he had painted the year before, no doubt under the combined influence of Cézanne and Negro art, in order to see what direction Cubism was taking under his influence. The volumes are less powerfully stressed, the rhythm of the geometrical forms has been broken down into its elements, resulting in architectural compositions made up of countless fragments, small, tenuous facets or geometrical shapes laboriously interjoined or superimposed. The original model was so thoroughly disintegrated, stripped down into minute facets, that the spectator's imagination rather than his physical senses had to make the effort of reconstituting it. This amounted to a new form of writing, a total rehandling of traditional spatial values and pictorial vision. It was an undeniably new style, yet one full of equally undeniable dangers, with the masses thus atomized, the form scattered into countless ideograms, the humiliation of colour, now restricted to a scale of sluggish greys; not to mention a certain aridness, complexity, even obscurity. It is obvious that Picasso must have thought out for himself a principle, and reconsidered a technique which pushed the

his progress in the austere and difficult undertaking which made up his very existence. Between 1909 and 1913 there was no abrupt leap into the unknown, but a prudent advance, a constant progress, a regular exploration into uncharted territories which had to be set in order and made safe as soon as they were conquered. Portraits and still-lifes in which the violin and guitar motifs often featured were at that time Picasso's favourite themes, which he tended to handle

more and more abstractly. We need only compare the portrait of Fernande (1909) *which he brought back from* Horta de San Juan, *with those of* Ambroise Vollard *and* Kahnweiler *painted a year later, or better still the* Accordion-Player *of 1911 and* l'Aficionado *of 1912, to be able to take stock of the ground covered. At the same time the colouring lost its intensity and was finally reduced to little more than a monochrome.*
Summer 1909—*Picasso stayed at*

analysis of reality close to the point where it becomes conceptual. After a series of nine pictures (1911–12) on which he inscribed the words 'Ma jolie' as a tribute to the woman who had lately come into his life, Picasso found a solution to his uneasiness in his first *Papier collé* or *collage*, *The Cane Chair*.

On an oval basis, framed with a length of rope, and among a few objects painted in oil, including a glass, a slice of lemon, a pipe, a knife and a newspaper, he gummed some corrugated paper imitating the texture of a cane chair. This optical illusion of the canework was set in a group of abstract shapes together with the first three letters of the word JOURNAL, which were an exact reproduction of printer's type, resulting in a work full of surprises which was to be the point of departure for the numerous *collages* he made during the next five years. It was really Braque who first had the idea of inserting some solid, naturalistic feature into the imaginary composition of a Cubist painting (in his *Violin and Jug*, 1910), thus discovering a new technique and new plastic relationships which many painters have since exploited in their own way. Picasso also began making literal copies of materials extraneous to painting, such as printer's type, imitation marble and imitation wood. His next step was to incorporate the actual materials themselves into his pictures: brown paper, wall-paper, strips of cloth, playing-cards,

Horta de San Juan (Horta de Ebro), where he met his friend Pallarés once more. Apart from the portrait of Fernande, *already mentioned, Picasso worked on half a dozen landscapes, including the* Houses on the Hillside *(page 62) and* The Factory. *Inspired by the austere local scenery, he reduced his palette to a range of ochres, a choice which was strengthened with the years.* Autumn 1909—*Ambroise Vollard gave an exhibition of the canvases painted in Spain in the summer. This* *was the only one-man show that Picasso agreed to hold in Paris before 1919. In any case he saw no point in submitting his work for the various French* Salons. *In this connection we must remember that Braque's work had been rejected by the autumn* Salon *in the previous year. At the end of October, Picasso left the Bateau-Lavoir and moved to 11 Boulevard de Clichy, where he took a flat with a studio.* Early 1910—*This was the year of the great Cubist portraits: The*

68

BOTTLE, WINE-GLASS AND VIOLIN. PARIS, WINTER 1912–
COLLAGE AND DRAWING, 18½" × 24⅝". *Tristan Tzara Collect*

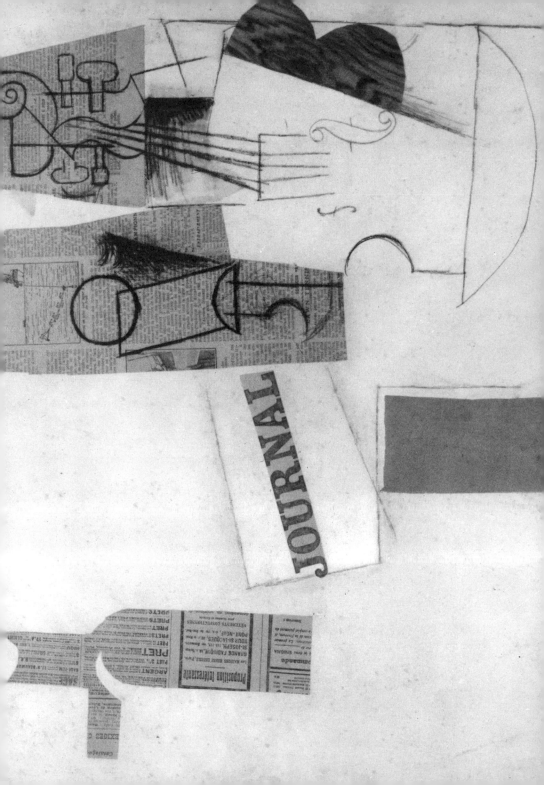

packets of tobacco, all kinds of odds and ends which he used together with drawing and painting in order to obtain surprising relationships between the immediate data of nature and the shapes he constructed or imagined himself. Among Picasso's *collages* we need only glance at such works as *The Bottle of Suze* (1912), '*Au Bon Marché*' (1913), *The Student with the Pipe* (1913), *Le Journal* (1914) in order to be convinced at once of the perfect genuineness of this new development. It had begun as no more than a scornful satire of the devices of imitative, 'trompe-l'œil' art. But it was very soon realized that bringing together forms created imaginatively and even the most trivial forms of natural objects could only serve to extend the painter's resources. Moreover, the Cubists were disturbed by the feeling that reality was eluding them and that their experiments were going farther than they had intended. Too much abstraction threatened to kill not only 'subject' but the physical attributes of objects themselves, thus reducing the picture to a mere decorative canvas, nothing more than a purely intellectual creation, inhuman, hermetic, plastically feeble. Malevitch, Kandinsky and Mondrián tried to close their eyes to this danger, but Picasso refused to take the risk, and the *collage* process enabled him to avert it. In a word the object itself, which had hitherto remained outside the picture, now came and established itself firmly on the canvas, so that

Woman with the Mandoline (*Fanny Tellier*), Ambroise Vollard, Wilhelm Uhde. *Each of these was a major undertaking, for the painting of which the artist needed many sittings by his models.*
Summer 1910—*Picasso stayed at Cadaqués in Spain, together with Fernande Olivier and André Derain. During this vacation he executed the four etchings for Max Jacob's book Saint-Matorel, which Kahnweiler was to publish the following year.*

These etchings mark the beginning of his career as an illustrator in the real sense of the term.
Autumn 1910—*Returning to Cadaqués, Picasso set to work on the* Portrait of Kahnweiler, *which shows the influence of the particularly austere and 'abstract' works which he had produced during his holiday. It was while working on this portrait that the artist brought into being, for the first time, the technique of 'superimposed planes' which, originating*

71

STILL-LIFE WITH CANE CHAIR.
PARIS, WINTER 1911. OIL AND PAPER ON CANVAS, $10\frac{5}{8}'' \times 13\frac{3}{4}''$.

from the example of African carving, was to enable him once and for all to break free from the slavery of imitation and invent a kind of painting in which, on a plane canvas, the various signs became plastic equivalents of real things. If he still needed a dozen sittings for this portrait, it is to be noted that after that date Picasso was never to use a model except on very special occasions.

Summer 1911—*Picasso spent his first holiday at Céret in the eastern Pyrenees, with Braque. This was the time when his canvases first contained printed letters which were sometimes*

drawn in stencil. Exploited for their 'trompe-l'œil' effect, these letters were the only 'real' objects remaining in works which were gradually leaving reality behind. It appears that Braque was the first to use this device.

Autumn 1911—*It is interesting to note that it was just when Cubism was becoming universal and attracting more and more followers, that the most virulent attacks began to be made against it. When* Le Journal *asked the critic Gabriel Mourey to write up the autumn* Salon, *he prophesied on 30th September that "Cubism, whether integral or not, has already*

L'AFICIONADO. SORGUES, SUMMER 1912. OIL, $53\frac{1}{2}'' \times 32\frac{1}{4}''$. *Kunstmuseum, B*

the artist was forced to build a suitable composition round the intruder. Smoothness of touch and texture disappeared as they were supplanted by ready-made features or materials. Irony and humour and the fantasy with which incongruous bits and pieces were deliberately brought together now replaced the ascetic and almost religious gravity of the Cubist discipline. The imprint of the artist's personality gave way to that anonymity towards which both Picasso and Braque had been striving for years past. The *collage* suddenly became, in their eyes, a kind of game which could endow the flotsam and jetsam of existence with all the attractiveness and almost supernatural charm which they denied to the noble medium of art. But it was a superior game, and one which was to have unexpected repercussions on their own personal work as well as on modern art as a whole.

Picasso used to take a sheet of paper as his ground. Then he would cut up natural substances—wood, etc.—and glue them on the sheet. These he surrounded or covered with lines and light shading. At first he produced some very graphic and airy compositions in this way. Later, as the fragments of alien material became increasingly important, the finished works became more compact and solid, finally acquiring an obvious and convincing harmony. In the *Bottle of Old Marc, with Glass and Newspaper* (1912), for instance, all the

said its last word: it is the swan-song of pretentious impotence and self-satisfied ignorance". Mourey was not the only one, for the majority of journalists came out violently in condemnation of Cubism. The Intransigeant *alone, in which the art column was run by Guillaume Apollinaire, and the* Paris-Journal *to which André Salmon was a contributor, defended the new painting. As for the reviews, apart from the* Mercure de France (*thanks to Gustave Kahn*) *and the* Revue Indépendante (*Roger* Allard), *they were all equally hostile. Winter* 1911—*The fact that use had been made, however timidly, of 'real' detail such as typescript and the like, was not to be passed over lightly. Once he had tested the practical value of this invention, Picasso further exploited its principles by introducing facsimiles of marble, wood and wall-paper into his pictures. Everything suggests that his aim was to beat the optical illusionists at their own game. To achieve this he went so far as to use a comb, a tool commonly*

objects were drawn except for the newspaper, which is actually a newspaper-cutting, and the piece of wall-paper stuck on the table. In the *Bottle, Glass and Violin*, which dates from the winter of 1912 (page 69), the news-cutting indicates the shape of the bottle, while the imitation wood suggests the violin. In yet another still-life the extraneous elements are used only for spatial definition: the *Student with the Pipe* (1913–14) shows a face which is mischievously suggested by straight lines and a few curves, topped by a dark béret made of gummed paper. Even if the *Violin on the Wall* (1913) in the Rupf collection, and *The Card-player* (1914) in the Museum of Modern Art, New York, are entirely painted works, the *realism* of imitation wood, newspaper headlines and playing-cards is reproduced with such accuracy that the two paintings give exactly the same impression as *collages*. In any case, they go to show how the new technique had so considerably influenced painting, that the hermetic Cubism practised from 1911 onwards was heading, by 1913, towards a more accommodating and broad-minded conception altogether. The meticulous

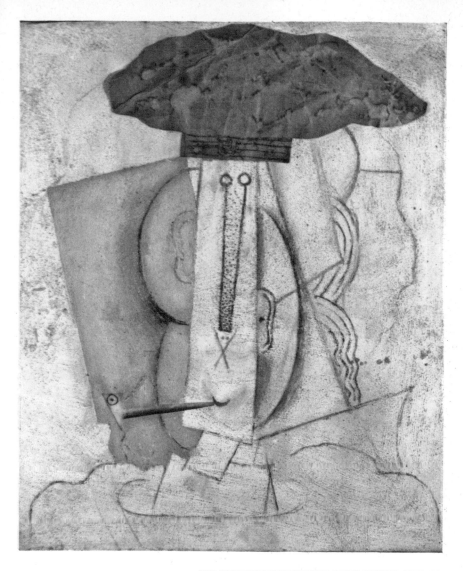

THE STUDENT WITH THE PIPE. PARIS, WINTER 1913–14.
OIL, SAND AND PAPER, ON CANVAS, $28\frac{3}{4}'' \times 23\frac{1}{4}''$. *Private Collection, Paris.*

TLE OF BASS, GLASS, PACKET OF TOBACCO AND VISITING-CARD.

IS, WINTER 1913–14. GUMMED PAPER WITH DRAWING. *Private Collection, Paris.*

arrangement of details, the breaking-up of the forms and proliferation of minute volumes which are all typical of what has been described as 'analytical Cubism' and which are to be seen in such works as the *Accordion-player* (1911) and *l' Aficionado* (The Amateur) of 1912 could not survive after the success of the *collage* technique. It cannot be denied that this new medium acted as a stimulus to Picasso's plastic bent, encouraging him to exploit the assumptions of Cubism in an unexpected way which led him to make fresh discoveries.

Just as in gradually shedding its super-added 'real' features the *collage* was transformed into a picture, at the same time when the raw material gained the upper hand the *collage* tended to become a work of sculpture rather than of painting. Thus the *Guitar* (1912) was made entirely of coloured papers; the *Violin* of 1913 consisted of a metal box which was prolonged, to represent the keyboard, by a strip of cardboard with the strings drawn across it; while the *Mandoline* of 1914 was constructed entirely of roughly carved bits of

used by house-decorators for graining. By virtue of a quite natural dialectic which perhaps contained a degree of playfulness, these daring tricks led to others, so that by the end of 1911 Picasso was adding to his painting not only facsimiles of real materials, but actual fragments of newspaper, wood, even sand and other such substances: these works are known as Papiers collés or collages (see page 72, for the first papier collé made in the winter of 1911–12).

In the course of 1912 Picasso was to exploit this new freedom in order to express his affection for a young woman who had recently entered his life. In addition to the two works of that period which contain the words

MAN'S HEAD. 1912
CRAYON, 24⅝″ × 18½″.

MANDOLINE.
CONSTRUCTION IN WOOD,

"*J'aime Éva*", this person has to be credited with inspiring the admirable series of canvases which, instead of her name, bear the words "*Ma Jolie*", words Picasso had taken from a song which was then in the fashion, and which had a refrain beginning with Christine's words, "*O Manon, ma jolie, my heart bids you goodmorning.*" Éva's presence brought about profound changes in Picasso's way of life. Giving up the Bohemian, nocturnal existence he had been leading with his friends, particularly Kahnweiler, he no longer waited till summer before leaving Paris. The love that now filled his heart needed solitude and withdrawal. Casting off a whole past life for which he had no more use, he left for Avignon. As he met some of his friends there he fled again, this time to Céret, where he spent only a month. By the 16th of May we find him at Sorgues, where he passed the whole summer and part of the autumn. Returning to Paris once more in October, Picasso took a studio in the Boulevard Raspail, at No. 242. However, towards the middle of 1913 he gave it up and removed to 5 rue Schœlcher.

The year 1913 was marked by no outstanding event, apart from his stay at Céret in the summer months along with Juan Gris, Braque, Manolo and Max Jacob. After being almost excluded for a year or two, colouring now reappeared timidly here and there. There is no doubt that the new possibilities opened up by the making of Papiers collés *served to quicken the evolution of his work on lines well outside the narrow principles he had so far been governed by.*

Summer 1914—*At Avignon, where he spent his holidays with Braque and Derain, Picasso worked on some large canvases such as the* Portrait of a Girl on a Green Background, The Man with a Wine-glass, *and some still-lifes, including* The Glass with Straw-bound Bottle of Rum (*page 99*), *in which, taking a hint from wall-paper designs, he gave the canvas a sprinkling of bright colours that lent variety and charm to an increasingly free composition.*

The declaration of war found Picasso

ARLEQUIN. CÉRET, 1913.
L, 34⅞" × 18⅛".
osengart Gallery, Lucerne

THE GLASS OF ABSINTHE. 1914. PAINTED BRONZE, 8⅝" HIGH.

wood. We can easily imagine the mocking delight with which Picasso assembled these strips of wood and re-created the musical instrument in his own way. Later on, and especially in 1928, 1932 and 1943, he was to remember his *collages* when he turned to sculpture. It can be said that Picasso never really exhausted all the potentialities of this device, either as a painter or as a sculptor. It was thanks to his efforts that the *collage* became established both aesthetically and technically in modern art. It not only modified his draughtsmanship and composition but affected his palette even more. In 1913 he broke away from the greyish hues, the thin, bitty touches of colour and his neutral, drab tones. The colour began to vibrate, warming up the canvas and defining light, shape and space all by itself. In *The Violin on the Wall* the red, ochre, blue and black are orchestrated with surprising energy. As gummed paper did not encourage or suit the finer gradations and blending of tones, colour came to life after a long period of sluggishness. The lively colouring lent itself perfectly to the sweeping but simple design of such works as *The Harlequin* (page 80), *The Woman Wearing a Chemise, in an Armchair* (1913), *The Woman with the Guitar* (page 98), *The Card-player* (1914). Laid on in vertical strips and overlapping surfaces, it clarifies and constructs and was indispensable to the new type of Cubism

and his friends still at Avignon. It brought an abrupt end to the exciting experiment they had begun seven years before, and for the success of which they had not spared themselves. There will never again be found such an unusual community of ideas and feelings as that which brought together such very different men as Picasso and Braque, Derain and Juan Gris; but not one of them could have realized it at the time. The break-up was so complete and irremediable that Picasso was able to say, later on, "When the

mobilization started I sent Braque and Derain to the station. I have never seen them since."

Thus ended an epoch which remains unique and exemplary for the high quality and strict standards of the works it produced. Yet it had not been without its disadvantages. Confined to his studio as to a laboratory, it is as though the painter stopped opening his eyes to life, so that for him the world was reduced to a handful of everyday things which for plastic reasons he had selected from everything else. Apart

HE MAN WITH THE GUITAR. PARIS, 1913. OIL, $51\frac{5}{8}'' \times 35\frac{3}{8}''$.
Private Collection, Paris.

that Picasso was discovering both in theory and in practice just before the Great War. No painter could have been more aware than Picasso of the excesses following on the teaching of Cézanne, even if it was with the best intentions in the world. Rejecting every possible submission to outward appearances, and at the same time intent on portraying the object in its totality, the Cubists might well be afraid that their ambitions and sectarian brand of realism might lead them into a denial of reality. After a series of experiments they found themselves faced once again with the dry dust of signs and shapes well on the way to collapse.

This might be dismissed as a paradox. No doubt. Picasso never tried to hide his realism. But he was realistic in the proper sense of the term. For him, being a realist did not mean reproducing the tangible world or making a sort of inventory of things, any more than it meant imitation, however cleverly transposed. What he aimed at doing was creating—with the materials appropriate to his art—a reality which would be the equivalent of reality as it is perceived, a reality in a sense more real than that of nature, a *mental object*, in other words a reality brought into being by the human mind. This is what was never understood by Picasso's and Braque's immediate circle, those pseudo-Cubists who with varying degrees of

from such musical instruments as the guitar and violin, the Cubists had a special liking for such simple and impersonal things as wine-bottles, glasses, newspapers lying on tables, and packets of tobacco. When they left their studios, it was only to find in the Montmartre or Montparnasse cafés the same old packs of cards, dice, advertisements for absinthe or Bass, or the same old imitation marble and wood veneers on the bar. By a perfectly logical process the still-life gradually became one of their favourite themes,

one might even say the only theme that had any direct relationship to their aesthetic system or daily life.

This was so much the case that when Picasso met Éva in 1912 he thought it was impossible to make a portrait of the woman he loved. It need hardly be said that for a man like Picasso there could be no question of remaining long confined to that world of mere objects, which he found so stifling. But through having learnt how to treat things exactly as he wished, he had gained a mental detachment from

STILL-LIFE WITH SKULL. DRY-POINT FO
'JERUSALEM BESIEGED' BY MAX JACO
(*published by Kahnweiler,* 1914)

success cut nature up into little chunks, thus relying more on the device of stylization than on the resources of their own imagination. A specifically Cubist work is, therefore, no mere image like any painting by Poussin or even Cézanne himself, but an autonomous object, a pictural fact, a creation which draws all its value from its relationship to the man who brought it into being. It is a convincing unity of forms and colours that are not just arbitrarily chosen but arise from and depend on certain rules and on a discipline and order of things which are far removed from those of photographic naturalism. All the traditional tricks to imitate space and dimension are cast aside; psychological expressionism is discarded; the object is no longer just seen from the outside and recorded by the retina, then remade and disguised according to some old convention: it is now seized in all its completeness and situated in an imaginary space.

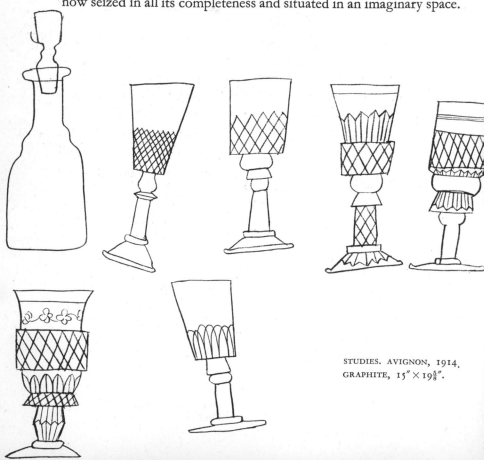

STUDIES. AVIGNON, 1914.
GRAPHITE, $15'' \times 19\frac{5}{8}''$.

A man of Picasso's insight had no choice but to react against an over-analysis which broke everything into fragments, the disintegration of form, the disappearance of the plastic theme in a maze of detail. He was too much of an individualist to be satisfied or come to terms with an almost inhuman, cerebral dryness and obscurity. At the end of 1913, after passing the summer with Juan Gris at Céret, he simplified his style of drawing, tightened his composition and regrouped and broadened his planes, concentrating his volumes so that they took on a consistency, solidness and fullness which had been impossible so long as he kept them broken up. Whereas the tonality had been monotonous and austere, it now became warmer and heightened, and combined with the drawing to strengthen the whole structure of the painting. This was the period of the *Woman Wearing a Chemise, in an Armchair* and *The Card-player*. It was also the period of those *collages*, reliefs in cardboard, wood and sheet-iron which all show an urge for concreteness and an increasingly sculptural approach that had been stimulated by the example of African art. For Negro art had more attraction for Picasso now than at any other time. He owned a *wohé* mask which did much to free him from a slavery to the solid block and helped him to discover a device that Kahnweiler called "the technique of superimposed planes": he thus came to make use of metaphors or emblems and in this way to find

reality which he was not slow in exploiting for his own ends. Attacked and even dismissed on every side, and the butt of the most violent criticism and jeers, the Cubists were forced to retire into themselves, and as often as not they took up a negative attitude. Thus, when Picasso yielded in 1917 to Jean Cocteau's request to do some work for the Russian Ballet, his acceptance was severely criticized by his friends. In his account of this event Jean Cocteau was able to write, not

without a touch of humour, "Montmartre and Montparnasse were under a dictatorship. We were going through the puritanical phase of Cubism. Such articles as may be found on a café table, together with a Spanish guitar, were the only ones allowed. It was treason to paint a stage-setting, especially for the Russian Ballet. Even Renan's heckling off-stage could not have scandalized the Sorbonne more than Picasso upset the Rotonde *café* by accepting my invitation. The worst

plastic equivalents of realities, and to suggest, by a few suitable signs, a surface, a volume, or the absolute unity of an object or a human being. Picasso's acceptance of African art undoubtedly helped to bring analytical Cubism to an end and involved the artist in the researches he so boldly pursued until 1914. For Picasso it was no longer a question of representing objects only by multiplying and dissociating their various elements, but rather by signs that would evoke them in the beholder's imagination, even if there was no close identification between the sign and what was signified. The hole which is suggested by the metal cylinder fixed into the *Guitar* of compressed paper (1914) is a projection which we see as a hollow, whereas the cavity in the *Mandoline* (1914) produces a relief effect. In precisely the same way the Negro artist can give a mask the appearance of depth by means of a protuberance or suggest relief by means of a curvature.

The Cubist group broke up during the first year of the war. Picasso found himself alone. That summer, at Avignon, he painted *The Small Table* (page 91), *The Glass, with Straw-bound Bottle of Rum* (page 99), a *Portrait of a Girl against a Green Background* and the still-life *Vive la France*, so called because of these three words written, in honour of his adopted country, on the objects shown in the picture. He was now dotting his canvases with light patches and

of it was that we had to meet Diaghilev in Rome, while the Cubist code forbade any travelling except from the North of Paris to the South, from the Place des Abbesses to the Boulevard Raspail."
This account is strictly accurate, except for the fact that the uproar had begun in 1915 when Picasso produced the graphite portraits of Max Jacob and Ambroise Vollard (*page 97*). Classical and severe in their execution, these portraits are sheer

masterpieces of which even the most realistic painter might be proud. They naturally caused a sensation. It seemed fantastic that such a deep respect for natural forms and such a complete absence of plastic devices should come from the same hand as the Harlequin, so purely geometrical in composition, that the artist had painted only a few months before. Then a strange thing happened. On one side were the artists or recent converts to Cubism who feared that Picasso might abandon

THE MAN WITH A DOG. 191
ETCHING, 11″ × 8⅝

shots of colour, and painting a bit of flowered wall-paper into the background—a reminiscence of the *collage* technique. The drawing became freer and there was a return to the curve, while the form began to show Baroque features. During the following winter he suddenly gave up that manner—which was almost a rococo mannerism—and went back to Cubism. This time it was a decorative Cubism in which he superimposed or set side by side coloured rectangles, tilted to the left or right. He used this method in painting harlequins, taking up again the theme which had so delighted him in his youth. Although he was not painting much, he produced some water-colours, large numbers of drawings and some engravings. He sometimes inclined towards a geometrical abstraction, and at others indulged in the most classical realism, noticeably in his portraits of *Max Jacob* and *Guillaume Apollinaire.* Apollinaire had recently been wounded in the head, on active service, and the portrait shows him with his head swathed in bandages. The lead-pencil portrait of *Ambroise Vollard* (1915) has a line and proportions as pure as any to be found in a drawing by Holbein or Ingres, whose skill he seems to be deliberately challenging with his customary impishness, in his use of all the stock-in-trade of perspective, foreshortening and modelling. When he was invited to Rome in 1917 by Sergei Diaghilev in order to make the costumes and stage-settings for *Parade*, a ballet

a mode of expression, to the triumph of which he had so liberally contributed; on the other were the declared enemies of the new aesthetic, all those who jumped to the conclusion that Picasso was in retreat and who thought it was their turn to crow over their opponents. Both camps were soon disappointed in their hopes and fears. The essential fact was that once again Picasso had broken free of the circle in which others hoped to imprison him, and had shown that there was no greater danger than being the slave of a formula, even the formulas of the advance-guard. Even the most timid of minds cannot regret the departure from the formal unity which had characterized his work between 1909 and 1914, when the same artist was to show himself capable of producing such works as the Seated Pierrot (*Museum of Modern Art, New York*) and the Violinist, *and in* 1919 *the* Still-life on a Small Table, *directly Cubist in style, and the*

THE SMALL TABLE. 1914. OIL, 51⅛″ × 3
Kunstmuseum, Ba.

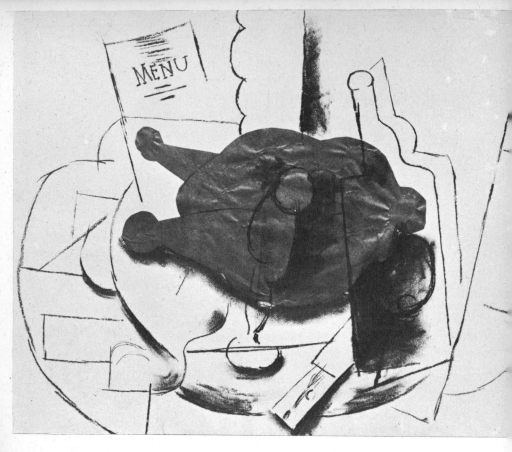

CHICKEN, GLASS, KNIFE AND BOTTLE. COLLAGE WITH DRAWING. PARIS, 1913.

extremely classical Still-life on a Chest of Drawers; *and, finally, the* Three Women at the Fountain *and* The Three Musicians, *both in* 1921.

October 1916—*Picasso left the rue Schœlcher for Montrouge, where he took a very suburban detached house surrounded by its own garden, at 22 rue Victor-Hugo. He lived almost alone there, as his friends, who were mainly French, were away in the* Forces, *and he had little regular contact with anyone besides the Catalan artists in Paris, especially Gargallo, whom he had known earlier in Barcelona.*

However, before leaving the rue Schœlcher he met Jean Cocteau. He wanted to paint Cocteau's portrait in a harlequin's costume and asked the poet for some sittings, but the portrait turned into a Cubist canvas with no visible evidence of Cocteau in it. None

for which Erik Satie (whose portrait Picasso painted in 1920) composed the music, Picasso drew portraits of Stravinsky and Diaghilev. The director of the Ballets Russes is shown standing in full evening dress with a top-hat on his head, while his manager Salisburg is seated next to him, also in evening dress but wearing a bowler-hat. The two figures are portrayed by nothing more than a thin, regular outline, without shading or qualification. The drawing is of an astonishing dexterity and economy and was drawn or perhaps even traced from a photograph. This makes no difference, it is so marked by the draughtsman's powerful personality. *Parade* was shown in Paris at the Châtelet Theatre on 18th May 1917. It created an unforgettable scandal. Picasso's scenery, showing stalls at a fair—a white 'flat' with a border of balustrades and houses in black and white —was greeted with catcalls, as were the dancers' costumes. The

the less the firm friendship which from then on united the two men led Cocteau to interest the artist directly in the creation of Parade, *a new type of ballet he had thought of in* 1915.
Once he had overcome all the obstacles involved in such a plan, Cocteau managed to persuade Picasso to go to Rome with him, to join Diaghilev. They arrived there in February 1917. *As time was short they set to work at once. The company had rehearsals in a basement of the Café Taglioni, while Picasso sat at a table opposite the Villa dei Medici, painting the costumes for the various characters and completing the design for the mock-up of the 'Managers' which he had in mind. Originally the ballet contained only four characters, the Chinese conjuror, the little American girl and the two acrobats. By introducing the*

MAN WITH THE PIPE. 1914. SEPIA, 12⅝″ × 9⅝″.
Rosengart Gallery, Lucerne.

costumes were certainly very strange, something like Cubist sculptures made up of cubes, cylinders, rectangular figures and cones fixed one into the other, parading under the arc-lamps. The audience took all this for an impudent Cubist demonstration, with the result that the ballet had to be taken off after a few hectic performances. But Picasso's first creations for the theatre are not likely to be easily forgotten. If Cubism was already on the decline, it was thanks to his efforts that it now became something more than a mere studio experiment or the snobbish cult of a clique. By stirring public opinion and giving Cubism such a social and practical form, he gave it a brilliant introduction to contemporary life. In spite of the failure of *Parade*, Cubism could no longer be ignored: from that moment it was to influence the decorative arts, posters, typography, ornamentation, even furniture and architecture. With the help of a few assistants Picasso had painted the curtain for *Parade* in an unusual way. Grouped into a burlesque and roguish composition we find the

'Managers' as visualized by Picasso —they were about three metres high and more like mobile pieces of scenery than characters—the idea was to reduce the actual dancers themselves to no more than puppets, the effect being to impart an odd kind of liveliness to the so-called Managers. This joke would have fallen flat if the reversal of values had not been turned into a kind of manifesto and acquired some symbolic value precisely because the Managers were constructions in space obeying the principles of the Cubist aesthetic. This amounted to an open declaration of the Cubist aesthetic's triumph over traditional reality, so that the first-night audience which hissed the ballet was not far wrong.

THE MAN WITH THE GUITAR. 1915.
ENGRAVING, 6″ × 4½″.

DANCING COUPLE. PARIS, 1916. WATER-COLOUR. *Roland Penrose Collection, London.*

jugglers, acrobats, dancers and guitarists of the circus-scenes of 1905. This is not so surprising, for Picasso's career is full of such restless impulses backwards and forwards, when he discards ideas and takes them up again, breaking, then returning to old sentimental attachments. In any case *Parade* left its mark on that phase of his output. He came to love the ballet as he had loved the circus. He married a ballerina, Olga Koklova, in 1918, the year after he painted her portrait in Spain. His future wife is shown in that work with a mantilla over her head and shoulders. He was also to become one of Diaghilev's closest friends and supporters.

After the war Picasso produced naturalistic and abstract works side by side, passing from one method to the other as if it were child's play to him. For instance, there was the *Seated Pierrot* (1918) with its almost conventional realism, and the boldly geometrical *Violinist* of the same year. At the same time he turned towards Italian Renaissance Mannerism (*Beach Scene*, 1918), only to leave it again and go to the opposite extreme: he created a race of giants whose figures had a swollen appearance, yet were controlled by a sternness of line that is characteristic of what might be called a 'classico-expressionist' style. The patrician dignity of his female figures, the fluted folds of their robes, and even the colouring which is not unlike that of the Campagna frescoes, all point back to the

Picasso remained only a month in Italy; not only did he manage to do what he had come for, but also found time to visit Naples, Pompeii and Florence. He did not cross the peninsula alone, but Stravinsky and Massine, whom he had met in Rome, went with him, besides Cocteau. A photograph taken in the ruins of Pompeii has survived as a record of this jaunt, showing Picasso, next to Massine, in the unusual attitude of lighting his pipe. There is nothing extraordinary in this and the detail would pass unnoticed were it not that the pipe had become a symbol of solidarity among the Montparnasse painters. Being one of the few everyday objects which the Cubists thought worth showing on their canvases, to some extent it had become one of the symbols of their aesthetic, and it was not only by chance that one of the 'Managers' in Parade, *the Manager in a tail-coat, was holding an enormous white pipe which was not really necessary for his role.*

96

After his return to Paris, Picasso set to work in his Montrouge studio, where he made the magnificent backcloth. Those who saw it will never forget it. This work is a pastiche, as the artist was obviously imitating the painters of those hackneyed scenes which commonly decorate the stalls of cheapjacks. The colours are fresh and lively and the dresses are lavishly painted. All the themes of the Pink Period are rehandled here, but this time with a hint of Mannerism which changes their meaning and gives them a spice of wit: thus the bareback rider on his horse; the Guitarist is also featured along with Harlequin, but their faces are no longer so melancholy. Even the acrobat's ball of the early works is recalled, adding its patch of colour to the foreground. We can well imagine the public's disapproval when they saw this curtain rising to disclose the Managers, and their feeling that they were being made fun of. Satie's music was not calculated to improve matters, for the authors had the idea of accompanying the score with dynamos, Morse signals, typewriters and other effects to deceive the ear in much the same way as the 'trompe-l'œil' effects for deceiving the eye in Cubist paintings.

The first night was held at the Théâtre du Châtelet on the 18th May 1917. There was an uproar. All Montparnasse was there, the painters in their pullovers and overalls, side by side with elegant society women.

WOMAN WITH GUITAR. PARIS, WINTER 1913-
OIL, 45⅝″ × 18⅞″. *Private Collection, Paris.*

ASS, WITH STRAW-BOUND BOTTLE OF RUM. AVIGNON, SUMMER 1914. OIL, 15″ × 18⅛″. *Private Collection, Paris.*

Picasso was wearing a red pullover and a jockey's cap. The show was greeted with whistles and catcalls, the performance ending in perfect chaos. Jean Cocteau has told how the crowd only refrained from lynching the authors as they left the theatre because Apollinaire, who had written the introduction to the programme notes, *was in uniform: wounded in the forehead and with his head bandaged, he commanded the respect of a naïvely patriotic public.*

The failure of Parade *had at least the merit of bringing the public into contact with one of the artists who in the*

99

ARTIST'S STUDIO. 1916. PENCIL, $12\frac{5}{8}'' \times 9\frac{1}{2}''$.

period he spent in Italy in 1917. But at the same time as the *Sleeping Peasants* (1919), the *Two Seated Nudes* (1920), the *Three Women at the Fountain* (1921) and '*Reading*' (1921), in all of which the figures are remarkable for their squareness, their enormous limbs modelled in dark, suave tones, he was painting still-lifes with a relaxed Cubist technique—such as the delicious water-colour, *The Balcony* (1919)—or in the fully orthodox Cubist manner such as *The Table* (1920). He seems to have put aside the idea of an exclusive system which could only hamper his lively personality. The truth is that the strength which Cubism had gained through fighting Impressionism and holding out against Fauvism was now exhausted. Cubism was beginning to stale, and had become the victim of its own technique of

obscurity of the Bateau-Lavoir had worked out a new way of painting. From this angle the performance of Parade *may be regarded as the first collective awareness of the new artistic phenomenon of Cubism.*

June 1917—*Picasso left the capital, going to Spain, where he spent several months in Madrid and Barcelona. He was accompanied by one of the Ballets Russes dancers, Olga Koklova, whom he had met in Rome and who shortly became his wife. His stay at Barcelona was one of great activity. There he painted a portrait-bust of Olga Koklova, wearing a white mantilla, as well as a delicately coloured harlequin leaning on a balustrade in front of a red curtain: this he gave to the city museum, where it may still be seen.*

Summer 1918—*From Biarritz, where he spent his vacation, Picasso brought back some delightful portraits*

SEATED MAN WITH ARMS FOLDED. PARIS, 1915. DRAWING, $7\frac{7}{8}'' \times 5\frac{1}{8}''$.

vivisection. Impassiveness, immobility, poverty of colour, thinness of subject-matter and a dim and melancholy glimmer instead of light—such was the price to be paid for the intellectual tyranny and ascetic discipline that underlie any exclusive cult of form. As soon as its heroic period was over the movement fell a prey to didacticism, dryness and academic formalism. Although Picasso continued making geometrical still-lifes—with tables, guitars and jugs—he liked to place such objects before an open window, sometimes passing beyond the window in order to paint the landscape outside. We feel that after stifling between the four walls of his studio he suddenly needed a breath of fresh air, and although he still obeyed a few Cubist principles he was quite prepared to cast them aside.

It may be impossible to follow Picasso's many changes of direction, his sudden tangents and sharp contradictions, but let us look more closely at some of the works belonging to that period of transition, such as *The Schoolgirl* (1919), *The Hearth* (1920), *The Dog and the Cock* (1921), *The Guitar* (1922). They still contain geometrical planes covered with a crude colouring, and sharply intersecting straight lines; but there are also curves, spirals and festoons which give the composition a fresh, dynamic quality. The stretches of flat colour are relieved here and there with stripes, dots and squares of paint. The outlines are embroidered with chevrons, star-patterns, saw-like

of women, notably that of Mme Rosenberg with her daughters, and the large composition Women Bathing (*page 116*): *the perfect ease and incomparable lightness of the line, the balance of the composition (fifteen figures in the most varied poses and movements), all bear witness to a surrender to the joys of life, a happy easing of tension, and simple contentment.*
October 1918—Picasso gave up the studio he had been occupying in Montrouge for two years, now moving to

23 rue de la Boétie, not far from Paul Rosenberg, who was his main dealer. Picasso made many drawings of his new apartment, all of them scrupulously accurate. Two of these drawings one dated 1920 and the other 1922, show his studio littered with canvases, stretchers and frames, all shown lying in that active disorder which was characteristic of him and which he needed when working. On the other hand, another drawing shows his sitting-room as it was on 21st

103

THE BALCONY. SAINT-RAPHAEL, 1919. GOUACHE, 14″ × 9⅞″.
Private Collection, New York.

edging, all kinds of ornamental work which express a youthful spontaneity on the part of the artist. It was at Fontainebleau that he painted the two well-known versions of *The Three Musicians*, which are the most important and significant of his last Cubist paintings. The first (in the Museum of Modern Art, New York) is the most moving of these, as well as the most solid and the most soberly coloured. The figures of the three characters are laid out in broad rectangular planes, while their faces give the impression of primitive masks. Only the harlequin, in the centre, with his yellow-and-red-checked dress and the curves of his guitar, serves to add a touch of cheerfulness to this sombre, eerie, hieratic work, whose structure bears witness to profound thought and incomparable craftsmanship. The other version (Museum of Art, Philadelphia) is painted in a different spirit altogether. The first two musicians have changed places, the pierrot passing to the centre and the harlequin to the left. But although the composition is more varied and the colouring

November 1919 when he was visited by Jean Cocteau and Eric Satie (page 125).

Early Summer 1919—Picasso went to London with the Ballets Russes company. Sergei Diaghilev had asked him to design the scenery and costumes for The Three-cornered Hat, *a ballet whose theme was taken from the famous play by Antonio de Alarçon. The music was by Manuel de Falla and the choreography by Massine. The first show was held in the Alhambra Theatre on the 22nd of July. Those who saw it have told how on the first night Picasso, with a mechanic holding a tray of painting materials, stalked behind the scenes putting the finishing-touches to the costumes. The fact is that for quite*

DIAGHILEV AND SALISBURG. SUMMER 1917. PENCIL SKETCH, 24⅝" × 18¾".

pleasanter, while more emphasis is given to depth and the decorative intention is more obvious, this variant lacks the dignified grandeur of the New York picture. The style of the *Three Musicians* was foreshadowed in the *Harlequin with Guitar* of 1918. Another *Harlequin with Guitar*, dated 1924, shows how greatly Picasso's manner had changed in the interval between them. They have the same theme, with the same figure in the same attitude, but the line has become much more fluid, playing round the contours, while the colour has moved up several registers and is full of startling contrasts, giving a hint of the bold rhythmic leaps of the *Three Dancers* which came later. The series of harlequins was not interrupted between the painting of these two canvases. Those of 1923, who are shown seated and with clasped hands, deserve some comment. The painter has now given way to the draughtsman and the Cubist technique has been completely ousted by a severe classical discipline. It is hard to see what Picasso was aiming at here, whether he was advancing or

ITALIAN WOMAN. PARIS, 1919. PENCIL, 28¾″ × 23⅝″.
Gustav Zumsteg Collection, Zürich.

a number of them braided cloth had not been used, but the most spectacular patterns were painted directly on to the material. Karsavina, who played the part of the miller's wife opposite Massine, has told how her dress was completed only as she was about to take the stage, and that she already had it on when Picasso gave it its final form: it was a masterpiece in pink silk and black lace, very simple in its design. As for the Corregidor and his wife, they were dressed in blue and black satin. The costumes for the minor parts were no less dazzling, and when the lively 'jota' ended, bringing the ballet to a close, it was as though one had watched some lavish firework display. It was a triumph.

THE GUITAR. PARIS, 1920. OIL
26⅛″ × 36⅞″. *Kunstmuseum, Basle*

retreating, what he was striving for or rejecting. It is hard to realize that the *Three Musicians* and the *Three Women at the Fountain* were by the same painter and produced in the same period, and the same applies to the huge *Women Bathing* in the Chrysler collection (1920) and the 'Pompeiian' *Woman in White* (1923).

It is apparent that in post-war Europe, when so many men were content to enjoy the delights of rediscovered peace, at least one man remained who was never to lose his old agitation, instability and feverishness. When Cubism had had its day or was busy dying, and he had withdrawn himself into an uneasy solitude, Picasso only set himself more experiments and problems. After admiring the Ingresque purity of the *Portrait of Mme Olga Picasso* (1918) with the perfect oval of the face, the slender gracefulness of the arm holding the fan and the placing of the other arm languidly stretched along

STUDY FOR THE DROP-CURTAIN OF 'LE TRICORNE' (THE THREE-CORNERED HAT).
LONDON, 1919. PENCIL.

The failure of Parade *was now for-gotten. There was nothing here to shock or upset the public, either in the drop-curtain with its glimpse of a very classical bull-ring scene, or in the sets whose ochres and black with pinks and dull blues evoked some*

Andalusian village, or in the almost traditionally Spanish costumes.

The same is true of the Cuadro Flamenco *two years later—a series of dances and Andalusian songs set to music by Manuel de Falla, the première of which was held at the*

108

the back of the arm-chair patterned with flowers, we cannot view the subtle geometry of the *Harlequin with Guitar* (1918) without astonishment. We are baffled by the hard, diagrammatic form of *The Bather*, a gouache of 1920, and the neo-classical manner of the *Two Seated Nudes* of the same year. 1921 shows even more diversity. Picasso's activities were increasing yet fusing on every side. He was painting, drawing, pastelling, and engraving the first of his 'tauromachia', and applied himself as readily to landscapes and still-lifes as to portraits and genre scenes. We must not forget that he was working on the *Three Musicians* at Fontainebleau at the same time as on the *Three Women at the Fountain*, the *Four Women Bathing*, *The Woman in Blue* and some 'Maternities', while for his own amusement he was trying to effect a synthesis of these two methods of representation in the pastel *Man and Woman* (1921) while also beginning the superb series of still-lifes which were to be sought after by art galleries all over the world.

Gaîté Lyrique Theatre in Paris on 22nd May 1921. For this ballet Picasso designed a setting that consisted of a little provincial theatre in red velvet, trimmed with golds and blacks.
But for Pulcinella, *a one-act ballet with music by Stravinsky (after Pergolesi) which was shown at the Paris Opera on 15th May 1920, Picasso seems to have been intent on less traditional forms. The action of this ballet was laid in seventeenth-century Naples, so he set about reviving the characters of the Commedia dell' Arte after a thorough study of their costume and ways. For him it meant recapturing something like the atmosphere of the circus as he knew it in*

PIERROT AND HARLEQUIN.
PARIS, 1918. PENCIL, 10⅜" × 7¾".
Mrs. Charles B. Goodspeed Collection, Chicago.

If we look closely at the *Still-life on a Chest of Drawers* and the *Still-life on a Small Table*, both of 1919, we can see Picasso hesitating between two opposite solutions: was he to follow the line he had himself discovered in the shape of Cubism, or was he to return to his earlier naturalism? But the questions have hardly been formulated before we see the artist facing other problems. If, for instance, the *Dog and the Cock* still shows Cubist tendencies and is rather decorative, the *Guitar, Bottle and Bowl of Fruit* (10/4/1921) has nothing whatever in common with the former of these two works: the arabesque prevails over the straight line, the composition is extremely compact, line and colour have parted company, while depth and space are obtained by a few superimposed planes. There are no more festoons, no patchwork of facets. Instead there is a sober richness, a bold reticence, a graceful austerity. Picasso was still trying to show the various views of an object simultaneously,

PIERROT AND HARLEQUIN. 1919. GOUACHE, $10\frac{1}{4}'' \times 7\frac{7}{8}''$
Mrs. Charles B. Goodspeed Collection, Chicago.

OMEN BATHING (BAIGNEUSES). JUAN-LES-PINS, 1920.
STEL, $23'' \times 28\frac{3}{4}''$. *Private Collection, Paris.*

but only the main ones. He had not forgotten the *collage*, that divorce between colour and line that gave the first *papiers collés* their value. In a word, the realistic emphasis is less to the fore. The bottle, guitar and fruit-dish are suggested rather than defined, and this is contrived with a few lines dryly traced over coloured surfaces, with an astounding ease and certainty of touch. This disunity between form and its physical context was to be taken up by other painters, long after Picasso gave it up—particularly by Raoul Dufy, and even more so by Fernand Léger, who made it one of the characteristic features of his style. Then there are two still-lifes of 1922, the *Glass, Bottle and Packet of Tobacco* (page 119) and the *Mandoline on a Table*, which both show the same overall conception, the same economy of means: but here the coloured planes are cut across by hachures which serve to break the monotony; they are horizontal in the second picture, but horizontal, vertical and diagonal in the first.

PULCINELLA AND PIMPINELLA. STUDY OF COSTUMES FOR THE BALLET 'PULCINELLA'. PARIS, 1920.

his youth, and he worked with re-doubled energy. Unfortunately some error in the dates and a series of misunderstandings stopped him from carrying out his plans. As for the backcloth, after working on about twenty gouaches showing a miniature theatre with its crystal chandelier, its boxes and scenery, everything was discarded but the scenery, which he enlarged to the size of the actual stage. This last-minute decision made for an undoubted success. Painted in a sober harmony of colours, we see the moonlit outline of a street in Naples, with the sea and Vesuvius in the background. In this setting, which is worked out like a Cubist painting, the artist allowed himself certain liberties that are not to be found in Cuadro Flamenco. The sea is represented by broad dark surfaces freely interspersed between the houses, which are cut up and lighted from angles that owe nothing to classical perspective. In order to portray the night sky Picasso added a frieze of stars framing the whole scene and tending to a large extent to confine the setting to a purely pictural area. Only the realistic view of Vesuvius in the distance served to open out this plastic world in which all the features were controlled by an imaginary distribution of light. For

113

EMBOWELLED HORSE.
CELONA, 1917. PENCIL.

THE THREE MUSICIANS. FONTAINEBLEAU. SUMMER 1921. OIL, 82″ × 90″. *Museum of Modern Art, New Yo*

these reasons Pulcinella *is one of Picasso's finest creations for the 'Ballets Russes'. It has none of the scandalous elements of* Parade *but makes up for this by a surer and deeper effect.*

After Cuadro Flamenco *(1921),* which has already been mentioned, Picasso stopped working for the Ballets Russes and the drop-curtain he made for the Blue Train *can hardly be called a collaboration. This was a danced operetta by Cocteau, with music by Darius Milhaud, which*

The green canvas in the *Still-life with Biscuits* (1924) is decked with leaves of foliage. The ornamental figures drawn over increasingly rich and vivid tones give the still-lifes of that phase, so thoroughly shorn of eloquence and constructed with a severe economy, a sympathetic appeal and touch of fantasy that were rarely found in Picasso's work before then.

The theme of the still-life placed before an open window often recurred. Evidently in his desire to increase the light in his canvases and to give stronger definition by an exact distribution of lighting, dimensions, volume and the inter-relationship of objects, Picasso used the window as a device for diffusing light over them as well as for creating shade as he required it. For we can take it for granted that Caravaggio's principle has nothing to do with this, as Picasso's light is essentially pictural and flows from his own imagination rather than from the window. The opening pierced into the background of the composition and through which we can see the balcony and the distant clouds or a line of buildings, as in *The Studio* (1925), has much the same function as the *veduta* in Italian art. It deepens the field of vision, giving an enclosed space the extension it badly needs, offering the eye an unlimited view of nature which is a relief after seeing nothing but plastic abstractions. We shall see how Picasso developed this device later on, and how every picture

was given at the Théâtre des Champs-Élysées on the 20th June 1924. This curtain, portraying two female dancers by the sea in an unusually powerful lyrical movement, was no more than an enlargement of a gouache he made in 1922. Of all the designs for ballets worked out by Picasso but never put on there is perhaps one which one particularly regrets not having seen, in which the actors were to be dressed like flies and to dance in front of a backcloth representing an immense still-life of vegetables and meat.

We must now return to the summer of 1919. While The Three-cornered Hat *held its own with the London public, Picasso left the English capital for Saint-Raphaël, where he remained till the end of the summer. There he painted many gouaches and watercolours showing a still-life on a small table placed before an open window. In these subtle variations on a theme Picasso was seeking some compromise*

containing a window excites a feeling of elation and light-hearted-
ness that make an immediate impact on the spectator. At other
times, to stress the dramatic tension in his work, Picasso used
an electric lamp to throw down a cold, colourless, artificial glare
from the ceiling. If we mentally cut out the electric-light in
Guernica (1937) and the *Still-life with Eggs* (1942) these two
works at once lose their austere beauty and indeed much of their
meaning.

In the famous still-lifes of 1924 Picasso was to attain something
like perfection itself. But were his efforts and exploits ever aimed
at perfection? As soon as he felt he was reaching it he kept clear by
some sharp change of position or clever parrying. This period was
rich in output but full of upheavals and undercurrents. He would be
alternately carried away by some overwhelming enthusiasm, then
sitting in sackcloth and ashes: at one moment dipping his brush into
honey and at another in acid, he vacillated between a cerebral,
premeditated form of Cubism, and the narrowest possible realism.
His work has always been an endless see-saw, a crossfire between
two opposite impulses, between the sway of the imagination, the
urge to create out of nothing, and on the other hand a desire to
respect both tradition and nature. "I don't evolve, I am what I am,"
Picasso has rightly said. And he is at the same time romantic and

between his recent Cubism and the realism which can be seen at that time in his drawing. The Balcony *which we reproduce on page 102 belongs to this series of works, and here we can distinguish the beginning of that blending of styles which was to lead Picasso to a more indulgent view of reality, and of which the culmination is to be seen in the great still-lifes of 1925. Returning to the balcony theme, Picasso made a lithograph of it which he used as an invitation-card for his*

show of drawings and water-colours, held from 20th October to 15th November in the same year, at Rosenberg's Gallery, 21 rue de la Boétie.

In 1920 came the first of the heavy, monumental female figures which have been compared with Greek or Roman sculptures. If it is true that, for these works, Picasso drew on some memory he brought back from Naples or Pompeii or Rome, it still needs to be explained by what miracle such bloated figures, with apparently so little in

117

classical, intellectual and emotional, a creator and a denier, a man torn by doubts and contradictions.

The range of Picasso's classical style was such that he could draw in firm deliberate lines portraits worthy of Ingres himself (*Mme Wildenstein, André Derain*) or handle pen or pencil with a Greek purity (*Women Bathing, Centaur Carrying off a Woman*), or try his hand at Alexandrian art (*Four Women Bathing*), and yet at the same time paint such works as the *Mother and Child* of 1921, the *Three Women at the Fountain* (1921) or *The Spring* (1922) in which he expanded or bloated the forms while still maintaining a classical purity of line. These monumental figures with their thick-set bodies, sunk in a sort of stony inertia, these impassive, rustic goddesses of fertility, all give out an impression of enormous strength through or in spite of their full faces, globulous eyes, dropsical flesh, their stillness and their expressionless features. But he was also to show these quiet giants transformed into deformed and agitated monsters. He thinned

GLASS, BOTTLE AND PACKET OF TOBACCO. 1922. OIL, 13⅜″ × 16½″. *Kunstmuseum, Basle.*

common with classical art, remind us so powerfully and disconcertingly of ancient sculptures? Not only are they far removed from academic antiquity as it is understood in the art schools, but we would search the Greek or Latin civilizations in vain for any work of such challenging yet quite classical proportions as the Two Seated Women of the Chrysler collection, or the Three Women at the Fountain of 1921. The genuine invention and originality that underly such a 'classicism' is nowhere better demonstrated than in the pastels of

Women Bathing which he made that summer (1920) at Aix-les-Bains, and from which anecdote and the picturesque are banished, to the advantage of design and line. We find the same blending of ancient and modern in the numerous studies of women's heads, two or three times the natural size, on which he worked during 1920 and 1921.

1921 was without doubt one of the happiest spells during that phase. The birth of his son, Paul, in February resulted in a new theme entering his work, the theme of mother and child,

PING PEASANTS. PARIS, 1919.

IL, 12″ × 16″.

out the torso to end in a tiny pin-point head and gave the lower limbs freakish proportions, for instance in the series of paintings and drawings of the *Women by the Sea* and above all the *Three Women Bathing* in the Chrysler collection (1920). In these he was thinking less in terms of amplified volumes and distended lines, than of creating a kind of fictitious space by no other means than drawing alone. Far from seeking to shock by these exaggerated shapes or his unbridled imagination, he was deliberately trying one of the boldest experiments any artist has ever attempted. One female figure, heavily lengthened into a parallel with the horizon, ensures both the foreground's solidity and the stability of the composition as a whole. The same applies to the second bather's left leg which stands like a massive pillar, while her shortened and bent right leg marks the middle ground. The third woman, leaping in the background, creates depth by the curve of the raised leg, the backward twist of the bust, the outstretched tapering arms, the flowing hair and

which until then he had only handled very occasionally.

But there were other reasons why 1921 *should be important. During the summer of that year, while spending his vacation at Fontainebleau he painted the* Three Women at the Fountain, *now in the Museum of Modern Art in New York, as well as the two versions of the* Three Musicians, *monumental works which achieve an admirable synthesis of the two streams into which his artistic output was then divided. It is disturbing and incredible that these three compositions should have been worked out simultaneously. They are quite without feverishness or the slightest sign of the haste that would betray any uneasiness: they show only the*

E. 1920. PENCIL,
′ × 8¾″.

BERTHE WEILL. PARIS,
SPRING 1920. GRAPHITE.

THE WOUNDED BIRD. 1920–21. PASTEL, 24¾″ × 18¾″. *Private Collection, Paris.*

READING. 1921. PASTEL, $24\frac{3}{4}'' \times 18\frac{3}{4}''$. *Private Collection, Paris.*

exaggerated narrowing of the head. This is a triumph of draughts-manship, in which, while ignoring the rules of perspective and the proper layout of planes, the artist's masterly exploitation of the possibilities of drawing alone contrives to build up an imaginary space which we have no choice but to accept. In *Luxury* (Musée d'Art Moderne) Matisse had also tried—by means of the arabesque alone—to solve this problem which has haunted painters down the centuries. But as he was too concerned with the harmony of the poses, and using elegant curves and a broken line, he had only touched on something which Picasso was to take up and develop into a complete success.

But the same artist who painted the *Women by the Sea* in which the expressionism borders on the grotesque, also painted in 1923 those charming *Portraits of a Child* (his son, Paul), the *Harlequin with Crossed Hands* and the *Woman in a Turban*, all of them works marked by their easy, fluid line, soft warm colouring and restrained but

ITALIAN PEASANTS (FROM A PHOTOGRAPH). PARIS, 1919. CONTÉ, 24″ × 18¾″.

THE ARTIST'S SITTING-ROOM, RUE DE LA BOÉTIE, PARIS, NOVEMBER 1919. GRAPHITE, $19\frac{5}{8}'' \times 24\frac{3}{8}''$.
Left to right: Jean Cocteau, Olga Picasso, Eric Satie.

assertion of the man's self-confidence as he carried out plans laid long before. Incidentally, there are no less than ten drafts of Three Women at the Fountain, *and they show certain variants. In two of them the seated woman on the right of the picture is shown with her legs crossed and her hands clasped under her left knee. For this figure, which alone fills half the canvas and gives it balance, Picasso also made two small separate studies.*

Among the other changes he made in the course of this work we note that of the central figure, whose position behind the rock, as seen in the final version, occurred in only three sketches. There are also about ten drawings or pastels dealing with either face or hands. Passing with the ease of a virtuoso from one technique to another, Picasso handled the same theme in two lithographs called The Spring *and* The Fountain, *both dated* 1921.

125

GUITAR, GLASS AND BOWL OF FRUIT. 1924. OIL, $38\frac{3}{4}'' \times 52''$.   *Kunsthaus, Zürich.*

In The Three Musicians *we are again in the presence of the undisputed master of Cubism. The two versions he made of this show marked differences in both the arrangement of the figures and the use of colour, as well as in the composition in the proper sense of the term. In the versions in the Museum of Modern Art in New York we can pick out, from left to right, a pierrot playing the clarinet, then a harlequin with his guitar, and a monk holding a score on his knees. In those in the Philadelphia Museum the harlequin is playing a violin and is now placed*

to the left of the picture: in the centre stands the pierrot with a clarinet, from the other version, while the monk, on the right, is recognizable by his homespun habit, with a cord for his belt. The dog on the left of the picture, under the table in the New York version, does not figure in the Philadelphia canvas. More complex, and fresher in colour, this final version has neither the severity nor the stark economy of the other, which impresses by its dignified generosity of conception. However, it is impossible to give any chronological order to these two

graceful naturalism. His Cubist paintings also suggest his desire for escape, his need to please after having so often offended. They began to take on a flowing line, harmonious gradations of tone, subtle inter-relationships whose charm makes us think of Braque. He now began producing the series of brilliant still-lifes running from *The Mandoline* (1924) to *The Fishing Net* (1925). If *The Mandoline* in the Stedelijk Museum, Amsterdam, still has a geometrical structure, surfaces decked with ornamental patterns and both the shapes and the space they are set in defined by a few simple strokes or by juxtaposed planes, the still-life *Guitar, Glass and Bowl of Fruit* in the

WOMAN, STANDING. 1923.
INK-DRAWING, 11⅝" × 8¾".

Kunsthaus, Zürich (page 126), is executed with less reserve: here the curve is uppermost while the colour is smoother and more closely related to the drawing. Thus two distinct techniques were brought together in the still-lifes of 1924–25—*The Open Window*, the *Still-life with a Slice of Melon*, the *Still-life with a Bottle of Wine*, the *Still-life with Classical Head* (Musée National de l'Art Moderne). These canvases are full of energy, elegance, freshness; they are rich, urbane and precise. Every one of them looks like a synthesis of the painter's earlier experiments and trials: Cubism and naturalism are found side by side, abstract images and concrete themes, together with the *collage* technique, the separation of line and colour, all completely fused and welded together and carefully heightened with a few sparkling echoes of Impressionism. The objects are set out in front of a window or against an artificial background of wall-paper.

WOMAN, STANDING. 1926.
INK-DRAWING, $18\frac{3}{4}'' \times 12\frac{3}{4}''$.

STILL-LIFE WITH MANDOLINE. 1924. OIL, 38¾″ × 52″.
P. A. Regnault Collection, Stedelijk Museum, Amsterdam.

interpretations of the same theme, as Picasso has made it known that he worked on both canvases at once.

1922–23—His work continued to be marked by the same dualism: on the one hand a systematic development and exploitation of Cubism, with all the variations it allows on such an apparently limited theme as a still-life; on the other the representation of the human face and figure by traditional means. If the year 1922 stands out

for its series of still-lifes in which, heightening the colour and laying it on in flat stretches, he broke its monotony by a series of parallel strokes, mainly black (see page 119), it occurred to him during his holiday at Dinard to introduce some new element such as fish, beside the usual fruit-dish, bottle and glass. He devoted 1923 to strengthening his classical style. It was a year of calm, during which Picasso drew and painted with unaccustomed

129

They all have the recurring themes, bottle, fruit-dish, guitar or mandoline, that provide a leit-motif round which Picasso played infinite variations. The guitar appears very frequently, and every time in a different way. Whether he makes it square, oval, rectangular, cylindrical or trapezoidal, it is always none the less a guitar, always different yet always the same and easily identifiable. To these objects he sometimes added a classical bust on a stand or pedestal, or fruits lying on the table. On the table-cloth, usually decorated with some small pattern, he liked to spread a sheet of music on which the staves and notation can be seen. There is such a sheet of music in the right-hand section of *The Woman with a Mandoline* (1925) in which the drawing takes the form of quick short strokes laid on flat stretches of colour. The volume is only suggested in this canvas, as in some of the other still-lifes of the same period, though sometimes the objects are still defined by intersecting planes. The figure holding a musical instrument is a characteristic feature of Picasso's human imagery, and has been ever since 1910, just as the musical instrument became an essential part of the still-life. Picasso never wearied of repeating his favourite themes. He was obsessed by the woman playing the mandoline, the harlequin, the musician and the woman bathing, as later he was to be fascinated by the seated or sleeping woman, the guitar, the fruit-dish, the bottle, or later on

freedom and serenity. All the canvases of that year help us to understand and share the unaffected joys of tenderness and peace of mind. Defying the modern prejudice which condemns any pleasant work as pretty-pretty, in rapid succession he produced such canvases as The Lovers *and the various portraits of his son Paul, every one of them a masterpiece, thanks to the perfect elegance of his draughtsmanship and the generous warmth of his feelings. Besides the portraits there was also*

a series of harlequins in the realist manner, which together formed an important exhibition held in the Rosenberg Gallery in the following year.

1924–25—These two years count among the most outstanding in the painter's career. With supreme ease and unfailing success he now gave Cubism some of its most famous masterpieces. But is it really correct to describe all these superb works as Cubist? His freedom of style was by

130

the candlestick, coffee-pot and lamp. His private life was always the focal-point in his work. How often in 1911 and 1912 he wrote the words MA JOLIE on his canvases and *collages* as he thought of the woman he loved! At that time his Cubist experiments denied him the use of portrait, but this medium became possible again after 1917. We have already mentioned the portraits of his young wife Olga. After 1921 she and his son Paul inspired his numerous 'Maternities', both classical and neo-classical, in which we see the child asleep or playing on his mother's knee. By 1923 the boy was two years old, and his father then painted his delightful face. He was also painted sitting astride a donkey, and writing at his desk, and in 1924 in harlequin costume. In 1923 Picasso also made a portrait of his own mother, whose features he copied with filial affection. We shall need to return to these personal or family likenesses, for Picasso was to meet other women and have other children. It is enough for the moment to single out a painting made in 1923 by the author of the huge matronly figures and of *The Three Women at the Fountain*—that is to say *The Lovers*, which shows a young man and woman tenderly embracing. Gesture, line, colour, everything combines here to give a reserved and graceful expression to perfect human happiness. Whenever Picasso takes up a new theme it is because he has been impressed by something he has actually seen,

now so complete and he related shapes and colours with such uncanny skill that the critic is bewitched and reduced to silence, for the analytical mind is baffled. If some careful observer should venture to point out a feverish haste behind this collection of triumphs, it is only because they bring together in a common impulse all the artist's oldest and most recent ideas, in a way which recalls the finale of some impressive drama.

Moreover, the same spectator would

no doubt have been astonished had he been present at the ballet, Mercury, *on 15th June 1924. This was a series of 'plastic poses' arranged by Léonide Massine to music by Eric Satie. Created for the 'Paris Evenings' organized by Count Étienne de Beaumont, this ballet shows signs of fresh preoccupations on the part of Picasso. The drop-curtain itself, which portrayed two harlequins holding musical instruments and which greeted the spectator as he entered the 'Cigale'*

THE WOMAN IN WHITE. 1923. OIL, 39¾″ × 32″. *Lillie P. Bliss Collection, Museum of Modern Art, New York.*

or because of some strongly felt emotion, or some experience in new places he has visited. When he started portraying fish on a table in 1922 it was because he was staying at Dinard. *The Fishing Net* (page 132) was painted during the summer of 1925 at Juan-les-Pins. The execution of his still-lifes became increasingly involved after this work. The line began to show some signs of its former independence while the composition was less tightly articulated. In *The Drawing Lesson* the figure seems the more disjointed as the table and stool are heavily and solidly constructed in a way which is emphasized by the use of reversed perspective. In *The Studio*, straight lines and arabesques are worked together into a closely woven general effect. Finally, in the *Still-life with a Ram's Head* the curves and spirals all combine into one movement which the artist has unerringly centred. On top of so many other problems, movement itself became an additional preoccupation for this untiring but eternally dissatisfied man: it was in that year that he painted *The Three Dancers*.

It is quite certain that this canvas was inspired by one of the rehearsals of the Ballets Russes. Picasso went on working with Diaghilev until 1924. He had painted the scenery for *The*

YOUNG MAN'S HEAD. 1923.
CHARCOAL AND GRAPHITE, $24\frac{3}{4}'' \times 19''$.

Three-cornered Hat in 1919, and the set for *Pulcinella* in 1920. As for *Cuadro Flamenco*, which was a series of *gitana* dances accompanied with songs and guitars, he had designed the costumes after the style of clothes traditionally worn by Flamenco dancers. In 1924 he designed items of mobile scenery for the ballet *Mercury* in which the sculptor's hand was again in evidence. Picasso is always full of surprises. He is driven by a burning, seething vitality that overflows in every direction. There is nothing his eye cannot see through, no undertaking to which he cannot turn his hand. In his endless quest he seems to be in search of some elusive truth: yet he discovers many truths, only to turn away from them and find others which also leave him unsatisfied. The closer and the faster he approaches it, the more his objective always retreats. He has scarcely ploughed one furrow before he has started on another. His experiments follow rapidly on

CENTAUR CARRYING OFF A WOMAN. 12 SEPTEMBER 1920. SILVERPOINT, $8\frac{3}{8}'' \times 10\frac{3}{4}''$.

each other, with Picasso tirelessly affirming and denying, at one moment aspiring to the universal, at another concerned with nothing but personal expression: he is for ever uneasy, restless, eager, embarked on some adventure that knows no end, but which, happily for modern art, has lost none of its challenge. He refuses to be bound by any accepted convention any more than by some revealed convention, even though it be his own. At the height of the period of those serene, impressive still-lifes, in the same year as the graceful, delicate *Woman with a Mandoline* (1925), after seeming to calm down his line became violent again, while his colour, which had been carefully orchestrated since 1922, began to clash in a painful dissonance. *The Three Dancers* (page 155) heralded the Expressionist Period, just as the *Young Ladies of Avignon* announced Cubism. These three frantic figures, needless to say, have nothing in common with

CENTAUR CARRYING OFF A WOMAN. 22 SEPTEMBER 1920. GOUACHE AND SILVERPOINT, $8\frac{3}{8}'' \times 10\frac{3}{4}''$.

the great decorative work that Matisse was later to produce for the Barnes Foundation. Picasso was trying to express movement through the extravagant forms and shrill colours of his figures. He was giving free rein to violence. After striving to find peace through order and decorum, his tormented spirit was suddenly overcome by his own lyricism. For him the dance was a soaring of impulses, a liberation of instincts, a trance; whereas for Matisse it was a harmonious displacement of the human body, a keeping time with the oceanic rhythm of the universe.

But he was not yet to unleash his emotional power, or to stress the caricatural side of his style. He had scarcely finished *The Three Dancers* when he went off in another direction. *The Milliner's Workshop* (1926), which is a vast monochrome composition, a network of curves and interweaving shapes, with its forms unmodelled but not without some chiaroscuro—altogether a completely original and strange work entirely governed by a broadly cadenced rhythm—was succeeded by several *Guitars* (1926) carried out in paint and several other materials. One of these *Guitars* is made of paper, cloth, string and nails (page 144); another of leaves, a strip of gauze, two hemp ropes and shreds of paper. These are pure figments of the imagination, ingenious variations on the *collage*, enigmatic constructions which cannot be explained away by guesswork. Critics have tried

Theatre, was thoroughly calculated to grip his attention. Behind its simple and deceptively easy externals, it contained all the elements of a new world of forms. A certain way of handling line as though it were a kind of handwriting, full of closed and open signs, which is also to be found in the sketches he made for the costumes, gives a mysterious, entrancing quality to this curtain. Indeed, far from merely defining shapes or so to speak imprisoning them in a strait-jacket

of outlines, line is used here only to suggest forms and, though without the slightest hint of artifice, to create light, colour, volume, and the surrounding space. Contrary to what he had done for Parade *seven years earlier, when in order to clothe the Managers he had relied on a solid Cubist construction with bleak sharp edges, Picasso now sought to express things from the point of view of their movement. To do this he created entirely mobile sets in which the shapes consisted only of an*

138

YOUNG MEN WITH MIRROR AND PAN-PIPES. 1923. INDIAN INK, $9\frac{3}{4}'' \times 12\frac{3}{4}''$.

unrestrained arabesque. Thus for one of the tableaux, 'Night', he tried to evoke the presence of a sleeping woman by means of a wire framework, inside which a cardboard structure could be moved backwards and forwards so as to stand out against the night sky, which was full of moving stars. As he thus gave free play to his imagination, we may surmise that the artist's aim was to interpret the very dynamism of the dance, only this time it was by discarding any form of expression that came too close to reality. From this point of view Mercury was no mere terminus in Picasso's work, but was at once a break with the past and a fresh start. With The Three Dancers the break was so completely achieved that there can be no question of premeditation. Painted in 1925 at the same time as he was working on the series of great still-lifes, in a sense this canvas was the painter's farewell to the classical world of the dance: it brought into an era of mildness and grace the protest of the instincts, the tumult and disorder of the senses. It represents the

YOUNG MEN WITH MIRROR AND PAN-PIPES. 1923. INDIAN INK, $9\frac{3}{4}'' \times 12\frac{3}{4}''$.

victory that was needed by the artist's masculine restlessness in order to persuade him of his own strength, and at one bound it hurled him into the centre of a universe whose coherence and validity only he could establish.

On the threshold of this extraordinary adventure on which Picasso was now embarking, it is important to point out that it had nothing to do with Surrealism. The very discipline of the works he produced in that phase and the overriding need for order which they reveal, forbid any comparison

with the new movement, whose Manifesto was first published in 1924 *under André Breton's name.*

Maybe the whiff of freedom and emancipation brought by the Surrealists might have helped Picasso to shake off some irksome restrictions and encouraged him in his bold experiments. But we must avoid attaching too much importance to Picasso's presence in the first Surrealist Exhibition which was held in the Pierre Gallery in Paris in 1925. *The Surrealists included his work on their*

to account for them by talking of Surrealist influence. But how could this anarchist Spaniard, always in revolt, always ready to attack prejudices and cults, remain untouched by André Breton's Surrealist Manifesto and the whole group's bold plan of campaign? But although he was not unmoved by the strong temptations of irrationalism and absurdity, yet he was even more on his guard against the excesses of instinct and had no faith in narrow slogans or systematic negations. His whole being was rooted in the realities of life, and even his wildest flights of lyricism were based on concrete experience. Surrealism was too literary and rhetorical for him, while Surrealist painting had an obviousness and a plastic poverty unsuited to his deeper needs. Although a large part of his work shows signs of an undeniable classicism it always bears the imprint of his dominating personality. In any case his neo-classicism has nothing in common with the neo-academicism of a Max Ernst or a Dali. Picasso is not metaphysical, like them, any more than he is a dreamer like his compatriot Miró. Similarly, when he was practising the most austere Cubism it was not as an aesthetician like Juan Gris. While it has to be admitted that Surrealism acted as a spur to his imagination, it is by no means certain that he was directly influenced by the movement or deliberately joined it. It is hard to see how such a man, who was always so ready to seize on whatever motive-power could serve his

own initiative, and one or two of them who owned paintings by him took it on themselves to exhibit them.

Thus we see the years 1925–30 as a period of trial and error, but also one of splendid successes. The novelty of his creations was then so great that the artistic quarrels which had died down while he worked on his great still-lifes flared up again. However, things had changed.

As Christian Zervos pointed out, it was not the same storm as before:

"Picasso had become a famous figure whose work was known to few but whose international renown went unquestioned, just as nobody disputes the importance of Homer although hardly anyone knows his poems." In addition to this, Picasso had a growing circle of supporters who ardently admired his daring hypotheses and who grasped the significance of a work whose first and only aim was to enrich the vocabulary of form, even at the risk of losing what advantages had already been won.

PORTRAIT OF THE ARTIST'S SON, PAUL. 14 APRIL 1923. OIL, $10\frac{3}{4}'' \times 8\frac{3}{4}''$.
In the artist's possession.

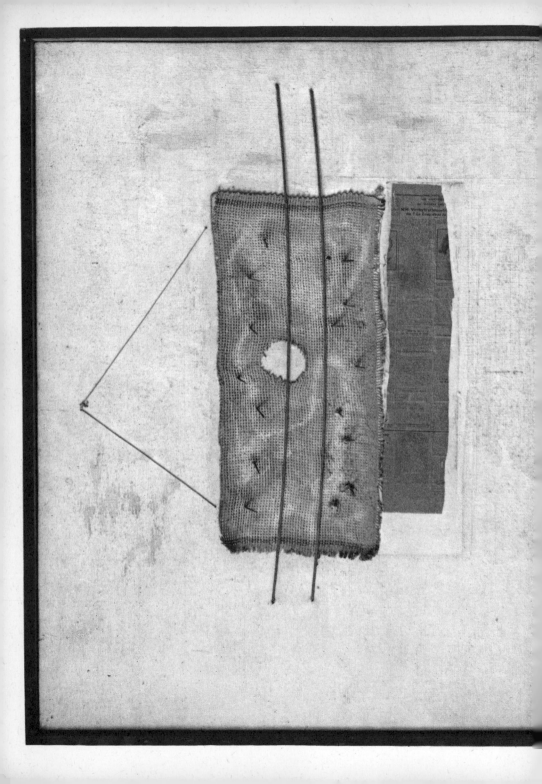

creative energies, or to absorb whatever came along if it really suited his purpose, could possibly allow himself to be dominated by Surrealism. The semi-abstract drawings he made to illustrate Balzac's *Unknown masterpiece* (page 151) are no more Surrealist than the *Seated Women* of 1927 with all their interplay of curves, or the tragically grotesque forms that he was drawing in the same year. The symbolic figures he painted in 1928 and the 'Metamorphoses' of 1929 were not Surrealist, either. Far from being creatures of dream or nightmare, or ghosts or phantoms of the unconscious mind, those forms which appear so fantastic and even diabolical are none the less real shapes, only they are reconstructed, portioned out and put together in an order unlike that of nature.

Some stress must be laid on the new direction that Picasso seemed (I say *seemed* because in his case nobody can ever be quite sure of what he will do next) to be taking in 1927, a year that was so rich in surprises. In his desire to avoid all definitions and restrictions, and to make himself and others face the most flagrant contradictions; led on by a horror of stability and unity, feeling most at home in the fluid, the discontinuous, the multiple; incapable of holding back the

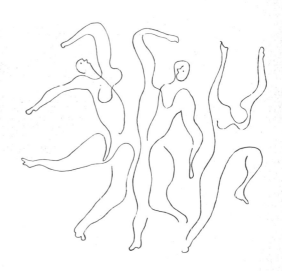

STUDY FOR THE BALLET 'MERCURY'.
1924. GRAPHITE.

swarm of shapes and images that filled his mind; tired of all the rules and limits with which he had surrounded himself, and refusing the temptations of success as well as every invitation to relax his efforts, he now yielded entirely to his own inventive powers. This he did without reserve, without transition and without reason, obeying only his own emotional impulse and the demands of his own mind. After the rich, masterly still-lifes of 1923–26, that great series of works all marked by an impressive poise, he let loose all the host of potentialities within him. These found their way into his canvases and folders in the form of freakish shapes, reversible images, charged with such a lyric tension that they would remain inexplicable, were it not that Picasso, as we know, always remained in contact with reality even in the course of his strangest adventures. Those faces and sleeping women whom the artist reduced to little more than a diagram are by no means the result of a mere aesthetic dilettantism nor of some arbitrary act of imagination; they are indeed human figures even if they are stripped of their everyday meaning and re-created after principles that have nothing to do with anatomy. They are usually very graphic, reduced to the essentials, and painted in uniform tones with little or no relief. Both signs and symbols, they express concrete and living reality even if they are not quickly understandable; it is, however a reality purged of all the associations

The stakes were high, and the leading Surrealist André Breton could write that "It only needed one man to weaken, and all we were fighting for would have been threatened or lost." 1926—Two works give an adequate idea of the two poles towards which Picasso's urge to create was to lead him: The Milliner's Workshop *and the notorious* Guitar *made out of an apron, a rake, string, paper and nails. There is no external connection between these two items, and yet they draw their strange attractiveness from the same fundamental need. They both tend to impress themselves on the spectator like absolute presences, like self-contained worlds that owe nothing to immediate reality. The fact that* The Milliner's Workshop *was inspired by the one he could see from his own window in the rue de la Boétie neither adds to nor detracts from the basic act of creating—with nothing but a narrow range of greys and an interwoven pattern of gentle curves—a*

147

of knowledge, and all the qualifications with which we surround it mentally once we have perceived it. In these works there is nothing left of our usual system of representation, identity, comparison or measurement. If we want to understand Picasso we must try to see his less explicable and more aggressive creations as a dangerous exercise to which he has fully committed himself, allowing himself only one rule, which is that for him rules do not exist.

The rather odd figures with several faces, painted in 1928, were not only intended—as in the early Cubist phase—to give a simultaneous view from several angles. His aim was, by fusing or opposing the different planes, to convey the greatest significance of form together with the liveliest human emotions, by the simplest possible image of a face or figure on a flat surface. During 1929 and 1930 he was alone in pursuing these researches, using nothing but line and flat colour when he painted, but taking the greatest care over modelling when he was drawing 'skeletal' figures according to artistic but not natural principles. These depressing skeletons, painstakingly drawn in charcoal or pencil, are the only part of his immense output that shows any trace of Surrealism. The gap between his paintings and drawings had narrowed to almost nothing by 1929, when calm, majestic figures began to appear in the depths of his canvases, like massive monuments. With their volumes stressed by

universe which can be justified by no reference to reality, other than the creative mind which had so deeply and deliberately re-thought it. On the other hand, it is interesting to learn that it was after seeing a sackcloth apron in the bathroom that it occurred to him to make the famous Guitar: this helps us to grasp the simple, mysterious power of an insatiable urge towards absolute creation, that finds compelling motives for a work of art in the haphazard events of everyday life.

Faced with these two works we might well recall Rimbaud's message at the end of the nineteenth century: "We will free painting from its old habit of copying and give it supremacy. The material world will become only a means for evoking aesthetic expressions. Objects will no longer be reproduced, but feelings will be expressed through the medium of lines, colours and designs, taken from the external world but simplified or controlled— sheer magic."

TWO NUDES. 1923. INDIAN INK, $10\frac{5}{8}'' \times 8''$.
Museum of Art, Rhode Island School of Design, Providence.

1927 *was a decisive year. Need we attach much importance to the uncertainty which was then noticeable in his work? May we suppose that he recoiled for a moment, as though in doubt,* when he was on the point of bringing his inventive genius to bear on the external features of the human body itself? It is clear that he could find no possible guidance or standards of

contrasts of light and shade, their simplified colouring and their isolation in an unrelieved space, they are almost like painted sculptures, closely related to the *Bronze* (page 161) and the *Design for a Monument* (page 160). Heavy, unmoving, solitary, Picasso went so far as to set them on a base or pedestal in order to give us a sensation of weight (*Woman Bather, Standing*, 1929). At the same time as this adventure into pure plastic form he began to take a keen interest in architecture, in which he was helped by Cubism. But he retained no more than the general lines and the bare bones of Cubist principles. This is seen in his painting *The Studio* (1928) and in his wire structure of 1929 and 1930, in which he invented open wire sculpture (which many artists are practising now) twenty years before anyone else, thus wresting from the architects a whole field which had hitherto been their private preserve, that is to say spatial creation. These materialized tracings, these constructions of wire and metal strips, were not mere playthings in Picasso's eyes. Kahnweiler has said of them: "In 1929 he was thinking of huge monuments which could be both houses for living in and enormous sculptures of women's heads, and which would be set up along the Mediterranean coast; 'I have to be content with painting them, because nobody will give me a commission for one,' he tells me."

It is plain, then, that painting was sometimes a second best for

HEAD. 1925. INDIAN INK.

INK DRAWING. Illustration for Bal:
The Unknown Masterpiece (Vollard, 19

Picasso, since material difficulties and the lack of suitable opportunities came in the way of his higher ambitions. This does not mean that the sculptor swamped the painter: each came uppermost at various stages in his career. One of the attractive things about Picasso is that sometimes he made paintings while thinking in terms of sculpture, and at other times sculptures that showed a painter's hand. It was in this same phase that Picasso—just as he had once inserted imitations of 'real' materials in his paintings and, later, those real elements themselves—now grafted all sorts of objects and utensils into his sculptures; for instance, a cow's horn, a funnel, a housewife's mop. As he had painted facsimile 'trompe-l'œil' fragments from nature into his Cubist paintings, so in 1929 he added life-size figures into his 'houses' which looked like women's heads (*Design for a Monument: Woman's Head*). He always longed to combine the most fantastic imagination with the crudest reality, to bring together what is usually dissociated, to unite contraries, to seize on what is discontinuous in nature and cast it into the continuum of the work of art. He always felt the same need to check the abstract by the concrete, and to enliven the concrete with abstraction. And he never lost the sly pleasure he found in shocking, astonishing or baffling others with his endless tricks and feats.

Picasso was now approaching fifty. No man of that age has ever

comparison when he had already left the beaten track.

At all events he stopped painting for a time, and returned to his engraving. He was gripped and even obsessed by a theme which indicates the problems his mind was wrestling with, namely the painter and his model, the changing relationships between the real and the imaginary. Breaking with an undefined, unspoken tradition, he deliberately reversed these relationships in favour of the imaginary, and

began a series of 'metamorphoses' that dealt mainly with the human face.

Summer 1927—While in Cannes, where he spent his vacation, Picasso was now obsessed with the desire to give more life and solidity to even the wildest creations of his uneasy mind. Thus he had the idea of making monumental sculptures which would be erected along the coast and decorate the promenade of La Croisette. To this end, he filled his notebooks in

THE BUST. NOVEMBER 1

PENCIL, 10⅜" X

created in such a fever-heat, painting, drawing, sculpting, engraving, dreaming of fanciful art while busy on naturalistic works, or of classical art when he was face to face with the Baroque; trying to rediscover pure volume—as in *The Woman in an Armchair* (1929)— yet passing, in another canvas of the same title, into a frantic linearism, and all this in the same year, even the same month. He was torn between calm and immobility and monumental strength, or pure abstraction, or the suppression of space or colour, or frantic movement, rich arabesque, strident tones, distortion and even deformity. These conflicting impulses came together and mingled in the 1929 *Women Bathing*, whose severe sculptural form is accompanied by a marked expressionism. During the next four years Picasso followed up vastly different lines of research, all at the same time and with the same intensity. The plates he engraved for the *Metamorphoses* of Ovid (1930) were classical in both inspiration and

style. There is a hint of Surrealism in his *Woman Swimming* (1929) and his *Acrobat* (1930), which look as though they were drawn after something kept in a bottle in a museum. His almost blasphemous *Crucifixion* (1930) is an outrageously romantic work, with its crooked drawing, its unbalanced composition, its cacophony of sickly blues, sanguine reds and sulphurous yellows.

After that date he seems finally to have abandoned geometry in favour of the arabesque, sometimes heavy and emphatic, sometimes nervous and lively. His still-lifes of 1931 are almost entirely made up of circles, ovals, whorls and spirals suggesting the curve of a jug, the roundness of a fruit, the pattern of an azalea leaf. There is not a single straight line in the *Still-life on a Table* (page 171), nothing but the play of fluid undulating lines and a blaze of colours; nor are there any in the *Figure Throwing a Stone* (1931) or the *Bather Playing with a Ball* (1932), both of which are built up of powerful volumes, just like the sculptures he was then making at Boisgeloup. The same may be said of the *Sleeping Women* (*Dormeuses*) of which he made a series in 1932: these women all sleep with their head lolling gently sideways, their arms relaxed on the elbows of a chair, or stretched out before a window or a looking-glass. In these pictures, all of which are transparently composed, the harmonious curves and supple movement together convey the languishing attitude of the

1928 *with a large series of drawings, all of them detailed and suggestive. The drawing reproduced on page 160, which he made at Dinard in the summer of 1928, is one of this series: it foreshadows those extraordinary paintings in which the artist at least crystallizes some mental plan or vision, even if he cannot see it achieved. This gave us other surprising works such as the* Woman's Head, *also called* Design for a Monument, *or the* Woman Bather Standing *and*

the Seated Bather, *both of them conceived as sculptures.*

During 1929–33 *the sculptor's activity was uppermost. The purchase, in 1931, of an estate at Boisgeloup, an old mansion about a mile and a half from Gisors, in the Eure, also favoured this work. Picasso turned the stables into a workshop where he was able to make pieces of much larger dimensions than before.*

After his iron constructions (1931) in which he was helped by his friend the

154

sleeping female body. But for the personal note he gives to everything, these *Sleeping Women* could well have been signed by Matisse,
the Matisse of the *Odalisques*—for it looks as though Picasso were
competing with him in order to prove that he was capable of anything, including an art of sensuality, the arabesque's suave beauty,
lavish decoration, the exoticism of rounded gestures, weightless
forms and sultry tones. So it was Picasso's turn to deck his wall-
paper backgrounds with checks and flowers or to give his figures
a setting of philodendron leaves—a tropical plant, dear to Matisse,
which Picasso had already used in some of his 1931 still-lifes and
in *The Lamp*, in which a branch of this plant frames a bust which
is powerfully lit and standing on a pedestal. But while Matisse
developed a voluptuous elegance and musicality, Picasso's impatient
energy erupted into the fullness and calmness he was trying to
portray. His *Nude with Modeller's Turn-table* or *Young Woman with
a Looking-glass* both show signs of an exaggerated and harsh sensuality. He painted them as though he was thinking not only of
Matisse, but also of Ingres, the author of the *Great Odalisque* and
The Turkish Bath, as though in his turn he wanted to paint beautiful
creatures, drowsing in the languidness of fulfilment. But a closer
look at his *Sleeping Women* suggests, rather, that their sleep knows
more of painful visions and nightmares than of the harem's wanton

STUDY FOR THE MILLINER'S WORKSHOP.
CHARCOAL AND WHITE CHALK,
25″ × 19″.

THE PAINTER AND HIS MODEL. 1927. OIL, $85\frac{5}{8}'' \times 80''$. *Private Collection.*

day-dreams. The arabesque that was at first so delicate and rounded, soon became harder and ended by twisting and writhing. The fine and graceful form became taut and eccentric. A memory of the Baroque distorts the sleeper's mouth, and the smooth undulation of the arm ends in an unpleasant angle.

Picasso was sculpting constantly at that time. With the help of his friend Julio Gonzalez, in 1930 and 1931 he made pieces in iron and steel in which natural and invented forms were combined, as well as some openwork structures, designs in space whose impact on the development of modern plastic art has already been mentioned. It was also in 1931 that he carved in wood the baton-like figurines, later cast in bronze, which have a striking resemblance to the Tchang-cha statuettes, although Picasso knew nothing about primitive Chinese art. In 1932 he had the use of a huge studio in Boisgeloup Castle, which he had recently acquired, near Gisors. There he was able to sculpt some enormous pieces such as the busts and women's heads with long, thin necks and protuberant noses and foreheads and with thick lips trembling sensitively, which count among his finest works. He was also modelling small reliefs which hardly emerged from the material, sketches he left unfinished so that they would lose none of their original spontaneity; besides these he made statues with rough, massive forms, such as the enormous image in

sculptor, Julio Gonzalez, he set to work with romantic enthusiasm, in plaster and clay, two materials well suited to his temperament. This was the period of the Women's Heads, with their large noses, which the public saw for the first time at the Spanish pavilion at the International Exhibition in 1937, and of which two replicas in cement are in the Antibes Museum. The year 1932 marks an extraordinary renewal in his painting. He then met a young woman with whom

THE PAINTER AND HIS MODEL. 1927.
Etching for Balzac's *The Unknown Masterpiece*
(Vollard, 1931).

cement which was on show in the Spanish pavilion at the 1936 International Exhibition in Paris. It was at Boisgeloup that he made the admirable *Cock* and the *Heifer's Head* in bronze, and the pieces made of a mixture of sand and bits and pieces of real objects in which he was applying the principles of the *papier collé*. Never did he work with such feverish enthusiasm. He made numbers of those strange faces with large, haughty noses, like New Caledonian masks, and others topped with a crest similar to those helmets seen on New Caledonian carvings, as well as some low-reliefs reminiscent of old Celtic coinage. He could not do all he wanted with clay, and sometimes he made drawings for imaginary sculptures, such as the studies printed in *Minotaure* in July 1933, which were not unlike the anatomical studies he drew in 1929. Then he left sculpture again and applied himself mainly to drawing and engraving.

Picasso's engraving is a pendant to his painting and often explains both it and him. In 1933 and 1934 he engraved most of the hundred plates which Vollard had commissioned in 1930. This series falls into several groups: the Sculptor's Studio; the Rape; a few engraved etchings inspired by Rembrandt; and finally those which deal with

FIGURE. PARIS, 1929.
BRONZE. HEIGHT, 8¼″.

the Minotaur. After a short spell in Barcelona in 1933 and a trip across Spain in 1934, Picasso, his mind full of recent memories of the emotions of the bull-ring, painted a series of *corridas* in which it is not hard to pick out the forerunner of *Guernica* (1937). Bull-ring scenes not only gave him fresh subjects, but also awakened that innate dramatic energy which strengthened with the years. He shows a powerful bull in the arena, bent beneath the blow of the final stoccado, shaking its huge head with a fury that only death can assuage; or a bull ripping a horse's belly and making it mad with pain before facing his own doom. The whole revolt of the animal against man's relentless cruelty is expressed by a hand as firm as the torero's hand wielding the *espada*. With the language of line and colour Picasso makes us share and almost assume the animal's pain on ourselves, a pain so exclusively physical as to be almost unbearable. But soon the artist passed beyond elementary sensation, leading us by the path of poetry into mythology itself, so that the monster's agony is in a sense sanctified in our eyes by its propitiatory, sacrificial

THE SCULPTOR'S STUDIO. PARIS, 2 APRIL 1933. ETCHING, $7\frac{3}{4}'' \times 8\frac{3}{4}''$.

function. The bull then becomes no longer the victim of some bloodthirsty game, but a ritual sacrifice. Art makes it more than a bull: the son of Pasiphae vanquished by Theseus, or the ravisher of Europa, or the creature of Ormuz slain by Ahriman. Quite obviously, Picasso passes so rapidly from the plane of everyday life into universal symbolism, from the most repulsive realism to the most sublime mythology. In an impressive engraving of 1935, rightly called *Minotauromachia*, the bull assumed the half-human, half-animal form of the Cretan monster. He is shown holding his right arm towards a lighted candle held by a little girl, who has a bouquet of flowers in her other hand. Between them comes a horse, with its entrails hanging through its open wounds, which is carrying on its back a female matador with naked bosom. The woman's sword is in the Minotaur's left hand, the blade pointing towards the little girl. On the left of the composition is a bearded man, almost naked, who is climbing a ladder while gazing in the Minotaur's direction. Two young women are viewing this scene from a window on which

THE MINOTAUR MOVES HOUSE. 1936. PEN AND PENCIL, 19⅝" × 25⅝".

two doves are resting. On the right, the sea can be seen glittering in the distance.

What was Picasso trying to say in this remarkable engraving? Was he opposing brute force to frail innocence, tragedy to happiness, destiny to hope? Was the little girl meant to be Ariadne, the female matador Europa, the monster Zeus, and are all the symbols reversible? Or what is the meaning of the gouache of 1936 in which the Minotaur stands holding a dead horse in his arms? Two hands are stretching from the dark mouth of the cave, and on the right a girl crowned with flowers is holding a veil in front of her exquisite face. Even though we cannot fathom Picasso's real intentions, this mixture of Greek legend and modern fable, ancient iconography and lyrical metaphor, give this engraving and the water-colour a high poetic value. The themes of the mythical bull, the disembowelled horse and the woman matador were to appear in many other works, and by no means the least important. Time and time again we are faced with the question, how Picasso can create, at the same time as his fierce bull-fights and tragic minotaurs, compositions of such classical technique and precious elegance as the engravings for the *Lysistrata* of Aristophanes, or paintings of such tender charm as the *Little Girl Writing* or *Reading*, between 1934–35? How could he convey such a sensation of child-like innocence with such a tormented

he fell in love: he was attracted by her youthfulness, her cheerful outlook, her bearing and her fair colouring. This new companion, who from then on figured in his work, bore him a daughter, Maya, in 1935. But first she inspired a series of canvases in which she is shown either seated or reclining, usually asleep, a creature of radiant, transparent flesh and warm sensuality (The Dream; Young Woman with a Looking-glass, 1932). *This was also the year of the*

large exhibition held at the Georges Petit Gallery from 6th June to 30th July. It was a particularly important date in the history of Picasso's art and its relationship to the public. For the first time and under the same roof there was a show of 238 works by this artist, including 225 paintings drawn from different periods. A similar exhibition was held at Zürich in the Kunsthaus from 11th September to 30th October.

1933—A book was published by

164

line and such crude colouring? More thoroughly worked out and constructed, the *Muse* of 1935 and its replica in the Rockefeller Collection none the less show strong signs of that expressionism which was to emerge at the time of the tragic events of the Spanish civil war, which brought Picasso sharply back to reality.

In his first access of avenging anger, in 1937 he engraved the *Dream and Lie of Franco*, a well-known album full of scenes of horror, weeping mothers, murdered children, fires and wrecked landscapes, prayers, oaths, bulls humiliated and horses dying, grubs with human mouths, all covered with hair, vampires drinking blood, animals disintegrating into worms, fish with obscene sucking snouts. Neither Brueghel nor Hieronymus Bosch nor Goya ever imagined such frightful images, such a seething mass of fantastic, terrifying creatures. The early masters of fantasy expressed horror by representing the horrible; but Picasso inspired this feeling all the more intensely by his use of broken rhythms, incisive line, freakish forms, harshly flouted artistic values. Bosch and Brueghel painted their macabre jokes in the same manner as their religious compositions, so that between the two groups of works the only difference lay in the actual subject: they had the same drawing, colour and style. Goya's *Disasters of War* was heavy satire, a fierce piece of documentary on the Napoleonic invasion: here it was a matter of a number

MYRRHINA AND KINESIAS. 1934.
ETCHING, $8\frac{5}{8}'' \times 6''$.
For Aristophanes, *Lysistrata*.

WOMAN'S HEAD. PARIS, 1935. OIL, 22″ × 18⅜″. *Georges Salles Collection, Paris.*

of real scenes, caricatural figures, monsters based on reality; the owl and vulture were as in real life, the vampire was only a bat, the 'proud monster' crushing human beings in his satanic mouth was little more than a dog chewing a bone. In spite of the painter's technical skill and angry protest there was little sign of either imagination or inventiveness. In Goya's narrative, as in Bosch and Brueghel, the old technique of naturalistic illusion imposed the familiar old rules and conventions. This was far from the case with *Guernica* (1937).

All that remained of realism and anecdote in the *Dream and Lie* was eliminated from this masterpiece, if we can use such a term in speaking of an artist who never painted for museums or for posterity. It was an external event that inspired Picasso to paint *Guernica*, as was the case with all his most moving compositions. The Spanish civil war overwhelmed him, filling him with hatred and revolt. Far from being just another work based on an actual happening, *Guernica* was the anguished protest of a soul tormented by the atrocities that set his homeland running with blood. But the work neither portrays nor describes these incidents, although it is the most violent denunciation of them. Nor is it an allegory. Apart from its title, *Guernica* situates the events it condemns neither in space nor in time. Subject, imitation, idealization, all the commonly accepted principles and all

Bernhard Geiser, Picasso, Painter and Engraver. *This critical catalogue which presented all Picasso's engraved works from 1899 to 1931 (257 items in all), and to which the artist gave his help, came as a revelation. It showed that the engraver already had behind him a body of work in no way inferior to his painting. His first attempt went back to 1899, a little etching called* El Zurdo (The Left-handed Man). *Picasso was then eighteen and was living in Barcelona.*

But apart from this effort his work as an engraver really began in 1904, when he suddenly produced a masterpiece in The Frugal Meal (*page 37*) *which cost him months of work. This was at the end of the Blue Period when the artist was still very poor; in making this engraving he had to content himself with an old zinc block that had already been used and on which some traces of a landscape can be seen in the background. Picasso was very fond of this engraving and had*

AN'S HEAD. 1932.
ZE. HEIGHT, 32¾".

the traditional devices of technique have been thrust aside by a powerful wave of emotion rising from the man's very depths. Modelling, perspective, foreshortening, chiaroscuro, all the conventional bag of tricks is discarded. Even colour is deliberately rejected, so that its prestige can do nothing to lessen or soften the picture's dramatic tone. Nothing but blacks, whites and greys, which clash together in a systematic tumult. The forms are freed from conventional appearances and have all acquired symbolic value. The savagery and injustice of war are conveyed by twisted faces, cursing mouths, a bird singing its heart out, a horse neighing with fear, bodies trampled underfoot by the Beast with beetling brows, and a Nemesis who can challenge the blinding electric light with nothing but a futile, old-fashioned lamp. Under these unexpected forms we can recognize the beings and things referred to, but by passing through the painter's own imagination they have lost their ordinary attributes and have taken on only equivalents that are even more highly charged with humanity and meaning. Terror, despair, cruelty, are made visible, almost tangible, by the virulent drawing, the frantic movement, the

CONSTRUCTION. 1929–30.
WROUGHT IRON. HEIGHT, 88″.

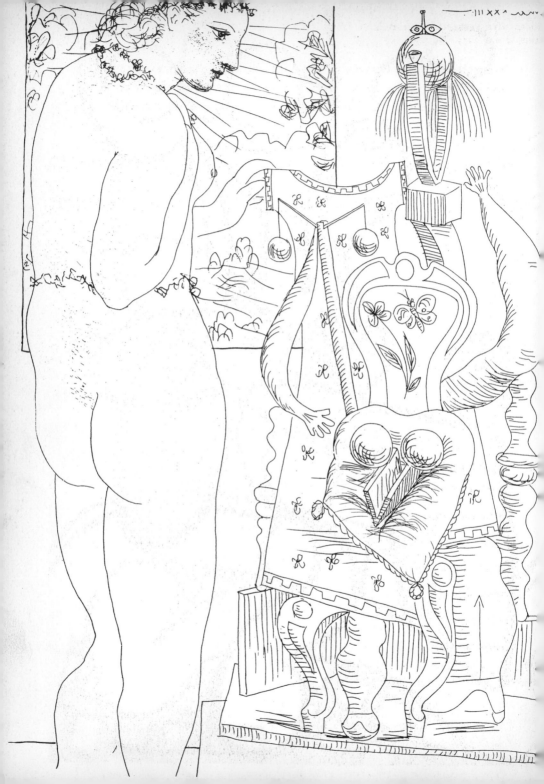

contrasted lights and darks. It was with line alone that Picasso gave evidence against the destroyers of life, and composition was enough to denounce crime, desolation and chaos. The figure on the right, with the eyes displaced in the face, whose mouth is like a gaping wound and whose chin points up to heaven, portrays a horror that was never previously achieved by only modifying the natural position of the features. The hand clenching a broken sword reaches the very limits of dramatic power. No human hand could express so much energy. *Guernica*, despite its apparent jumble of lines and planes, its confined space in which insane destructiveness and indignation and the demand for justice are all brought together, is none the less a work that was profoundly willed, thought over, calculated in its every detail. Discipline restrains excess, logic governs disorder, intelligence directs passion. That is why it can be said that here, for the first and perhaps the last time, Picasso imposed a style on his expressionism: thus he solved what seemed an unanswerable problem, how to give classical form to a work which overflows the classical bounds through the violence of its effusiveness and forms.

Even after *Guernica* had reached the Spanish pavilion at the Paris

some prints taken on cream-laid paper by the printer Auguste Delâtre, which he gave to his friends. The following year he engraved a series of etchings and dry-points entitled The Acrobats, *which have the same themes as were then figuring in his paintings. These plates are now recognized classics and are much sought-after. We note particularly the* Woman's Head in Profile (*page 48*), The Acrobats (*page 52*), The Bath *and the* Acrobat's Family, with a Monkey, *and finally the sensual, suggestive* Salome (*page 49*) *in which Herod was impersonated by*

BRONZE HEAD. 1932.
HEIGHT, 28".

exhibition, Picasso continued drawing, painting and engraving the main features to be found in the painting. The bull appeared frequently in his still-lifes, etchings and sculptures. From June 1937 onwards he painted large numbers of 'weeping women' in which his increasingly free expressionism took the form of broken lines, sharp angles, vivid reds, gaudy yellows and acid greens. The tears gradually spread like scars over the whole face, and finally over the whole composition. In the spring of 1938, with pen or coloured chalks, he made a series of female figures, full length or bust, in which distortion was taken beyond any rational limits. Deeply grooved faces covered with thorns and pins, topped with fantastic hats, or else stiff dislocated bodies now appeared in his sketch-books, streaked this way and that with lines and blots. The following summer, at Mougins, this intricate, chaotic drawing became simplified but no more attractive, he now made the series of *Men or Women*

STILL-LIFE. 1931. OIL, 50″ × 76″.
Morton D. May Collection, St. Louis, U.S.A.

with Lollipops, hideous creatures all scored across with hard thick lines which look as though they were made of plaited straw like the hats they are wearing. Whether done with the brush or in coloured crayons they recall the New Hebrides fibre masks, or the New Britain masks in bark which were used for driving away evil spirits. We cannot help thinking of Van Gogh's Camargue cow-herd, though even in his worst fits of insanity Van Gogh never produced such scarecrows as these.

In 1937 Picasso also started his long series of portraits, if we can so term these very free interpretations of the human face. Yet each of the *Seated Women* he has painted since then is undoubtedly the image of some woman he has loved, or some little girl whose charm has touched his heart. But these images are as far removed from the model as a novel is from material reality. We think of some grimace thrown back by a twisted mirror at a fair, which automatically makes people laugh: only with this difference, that a Picasso portrait does not excite laughter, even if it is full of gentleness like that *Seated Woman* which has such a light touch that the colours have the transparency of pastel (it was the mother of Maya, Picasso's first daughter; see page 194), or like the *Portrait of Dora Maar* of the same year (1937). This gallery of portraits could be divided into two groups: those which in spite of the extreme of transposition express

one of the circus-men who often featured in his paintings. These were also cut on the reverse side of used blocks, and were printed by Delâtre and put up for sale by Clovis Sagot, who had enormous difficulty in selling them. Vollard bought the metal plates in 1913 and had them reinforced with steel, printing them together with The Frugal Meal *in a limited edition of 279 copies. From 1907 to 1917 Picasso engraved about thirty plates, including the* Man with a Dog

(1914), which was only published in 1930. Among this number are the seven etchings—two groups of four and three—which at Kahnweiler's request he made for illustrating two books by Max Jacob, Saint-Matorel *(1911) and* Jerusalem Besieged *(1913). 1919 is an important date for any study of Picasso's engravings, for this was when he made his first lithograph,* The Window at Saint-Raphael. *He liked the process, which was new to him, and between 1919 and 1930*

176

MINOTAUR CARRYING A DYING HORSE. PARIS, 6 MAY 1936. INDIAN INK AND WASH, 20″ × 25¾″.

such agreeable feelings as admiration, protectiveness, indulgence or

he made about thirty plates. But this did not tempt him to give up the other engraving processes: etching and dry-point. But whatever techniques he used his preference for pure line only increased, whether he drew with litho-grapher's pencil or dry-point, his portraits of Raymond Radiguet (1920), Paul Valéry (1920), André Salmon (1921), Pierre Reverdy

(1922), Max Jacob (1922) *and* André Breton (1923), *or rehandled with a rare economy the subjects which also interested him as a painter, such as bathing women, a mother and child, the Three Graces or a woman dressing her hair. In 1927 Vollard introduced him to the engraver Louis Fort, "an engraver of long experience, who had a collection of marvellous old Japanese*

178

tenderness; and those on the other hand which are completely un-sentimental, tortured shapes and colours affected by an unquiet, demanding temperament that is capable of but little serenity or resignation. This is the case with the *Girl with a Cock* (1938) and the numerous 'Harpies' which followed it, and with all those women that some drunken sawbones seems to have carved up and clumsily stitched together, or on which some boisterous imagination has been let loose in order to ridicule and shame the sacred forms of life. Whether Picasso was freeing some sadistic urge in these mocking hybridizations, or ridding himself of some obsession through a loose form of art, the Baroque tendency that was first liberated by the events in Spain, then stimulated by the defeat and occupation of France, became a regular feature in his manner. The portraits in which, according to the convention he had already discovered, the face is shown simultaneously from the front and in profile, in which the eyes, nose and mouth are impudently arranged in a way which flouts anatomy, and in which women are afflicted with repulsive deformities such as squints, necrosis, lupus and tumours, are an offence to nature, an insult to reason and good taste. But Picasso was, or thought himself, above what we call taste, reason and nature. For such a man, art cannot be merely the application of a canon of beauty any more than a copy of reality. As he said, in one of his rare

prints". Picasso made a series of etchings on the theme of the Painter and his Model. *Thirteen of these plates were used by Vollard to illustrate Balzac's* The Unknown Masterpiece *which was published in 1931. In the same year appeared Ovid's* Metamorphoses, *published by Albert Skira and illustrated with thirty etchings in which the light is remarkable. Drawn directly on the block without the slightest hesitation or the least hint of a second-thought,*

they are works of supreme mastery and precision. There is perhaps less daring and mystery in the six etchings he made in 1934 for the Lysistrata *of Aristophanes, though they are also very beautiful. In 1933–34 he enriched his engraved work with a series of 100 plates, even more marvellous than those he had already done, if that is possible, which forms the most surprising element in all his production. This series, which was commissioned by Vollard, with the exception of a*

179

Overleaf:
GUERNICA. PARIS, MAY 1937.
OIL, 140⅜″ × 312¾″.

pronouncements, "the painter makes paintings in the urgent need to discharge his own emotions and visions". But perhaps it is also the result of some malicious need to mystify the public? In any case Picasso has always had the urge to strengthen his grasp on things, and to use or even abuse all the liberties he claims for the artist. He has used what is, traditionally, the most realistic medium—for the portrait is, by definition, the image of a person—with an impertinence that deliberately scorns long-established conventions, in order to scorn the work of the Creator, to become a creator himself and dictate his own laws; then, once he has imposed those laws, to announce new ones which he betrays unscrupulously whenever he feels like it. He is out to modify the universal order and complete it and enrich it, to restore it in all its original grandeur. In this he was

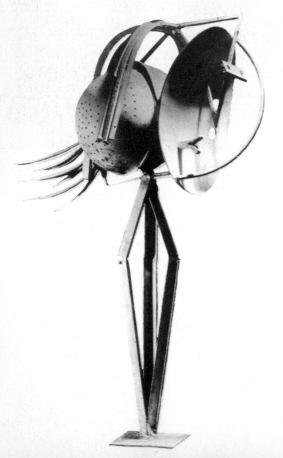

WROUGHT-IRON SCULPTURE.
1931. HEIGHT, 40".

STILL-LIFE WITH LEMONS AND ORANGES. 1936. OIL, $21\frac{5}{8}'' \times 26''$. *Musée d'Art Moderne, Paris.*

few odd plates, may be grouped into four main themes: The Sculptor's Studio, *made up of forty-five plates executed in two phases (March–May* 1933 *and January–March* 1934); The Minotaur, *eleven plates, May–June* 1933; The Rape, *five plates, April and November* 1933; Rembrandt and his Betrothed, *four plates, September–October* 1934. *Whether they arise from his own caprice—as with the Rembrandt series—or from some everyday experi-* ence, *as with the Sculptor sequence, or from the very depths of the subconscious as with* The Rape *and* The Minotaur, *these plates show, more than any others, a man at once inspired by and a prey to the dazzling inspirations and the uncontrollable demands of his inner daemon.*

Summer 1934—*From a voyage in Spain, which took him from San Sebastian to Madrid and Toledo, the Escorial and Barcelona, he brought back memories of bull-fight scenes*

behaving not unlike the Egyptians, who in order to explain the human body showed the lower limbs in profile and the shoulders frontally, and gave a front view of the eye in a profiled face—or like the Negro artists who interchange the reliefs and hollows of the face in their masks. If they could do so there is no reason why Picasso should not use similar devices in rearranging natural features, showing their inner structure, or presenting the whole range of viewpoints.

If, for instance, we examine the *Seated Woman* (page 194) of 1937, which is fluently painted with the tip of the brush; or the *Woman Leaning on Her Elbow* (page 192) of the same year, but harshly painted in 'ripolin' paint; or else the alert face of young *Maya* (1938), we see that at that time the artist was pursuing similar ends to those in his early Cubist compositions. But although he still tried to show things that cannot all be seen at once, that intention is all they have in common with the *Seated Woman* of 1909 or the *Girl with a Mandoline* of 1910. Unlike the latter painting, instead of being made up of angles, broken planes and geometrical volumes, the post-1937 *Seated*

REMBRANDT WITH A YOUNG WOMAN. PARIS, 18 FEBRUARY 1934. ETCHING, $5\frac{1}{2}'' \times 8\frac{1}{4}''$.

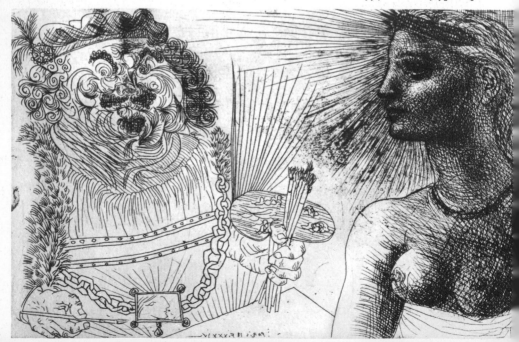

Women are essentially composed of curves, undulating lines, modelled reliefs and primary colours. In the background the straight lines define the small interior in which the figure is set. But to return to the *Seated Woman* of 1937 with its pastel tones, and the portrait of *Maya* of 1938, as well as the first portraits of Dora Maar, a newcomer into his life. By what paradox can such delicacy and ardour be suggested in such disintegrated faces, twisted arms and boneless hands? The *Portrait of Sabartés*, in which Picasso's close friend is portrayed as a sixteenth-century hidalgo, has nothing perverse or unpleasant about it, either, despite the double presentation of the head, the lack of any axis, the empty orbit of the eye and the displacing of the nose (page 203). The softness of the contours, lightness of colouring and a certain humour in the contrast between the toque and ruff and the extraordinary face attract rather than shock the spectator.

The same can hardly be said of the horrible *Woman with a Cat* (1937) or the hideous *Woman on a Sofa* (1939) or the obscene *Woman Dressing Her Hair*, painted at Royan in 1940. Can the search for

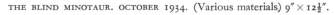

THE BLIND MINOTAUR. OCTOBER 1934. (Various materials) 9″ × 12½″.

THE MUSE. PARIS. 21 JANUARY 1935. OIL, 52″ × 66″. *Musée d'Art Moderne, Paris.*

which he crystallized in about a dozen canvases after his return to Boisgeloup in the autumn. Owing to their extreme violence and cruelty these works offered an unexpected note of warning to a world that was still relatively calm and had abandoned itself to the normal pleasures of life.

1935—For the first time in thirty years Picasso remained in the capital in the summer. His life was then darkened by divorce proceedings which came to nothing. He was working very little and it seems as though for a time he found little to live for. Apart from The Muse (January) and its replica (February) he spent his time almost entirely on engraving (The Minotauromachia, 1935) and on poetry, for he had been writing ever since his last stay at Boisgeloup. After keeping this new hobby-horse a secret for some

plasticity, significant form, be enough justification for such insults to harmony and decorum? Has Picasso's world any connection with the world of caprice and disillusion to be found in Greek mythology, the Teratology of the East, the chimaerae of medieval Christian art, the puzzle-pictures of the sixteenth-century Italian Mannerists, the supernatural creatures invented by William Blake, Odilon Redon or Max Ernst? Religious symbols, revelations of the beyond, allegorical throw-backs, ethereal dreams, the dehumanized inventions of Mersenne and Niceron, the ambiguous *divertimenti* of Mannerist art which lavish all their ingenuity on including several forms in one—all these are nothing but games, amusements, idle speculations, whereas Picasso's experiments were for him an absolute necessity. He has always fully committed himself to them and in them, with all his instincts, desires, impulses, his longing for adventure and danger. "Painting", he has said, "goes through phases of fullness and emptiness. That is the whole secret of art." Thus the sincerity, seriousness and genuineness of his most displeasing creations finally convince us, once we have recovered from our first recoil. Perhaps it would be otherwise if our ways of feeling and thinking had not already yielded before the sudden revelation of so many strange forms and shapes that our civilization has discovered. The terrifying Tantric god, the grimacing Borneo mask, the dark

time, Picasso decided to mention it to his friend Sabartés, who at his request came to stay with him and became his secretary. Some of these poems were published in February 1936 in a special issue of the Cahiers d'Art.
1936—From January to May there were three exhibitions, which once more brought Picasso's name to the forefront of the world of art. In Spain, where nothing of his had been seen since 1902, a retrospective show of his work was organized by the 'Friends of the New Arts', in Barcelona in January, then at Bilbao in March and Madrid in May. In France the Renou and Colle Gallery presented a collection of his drawings from 14th February onwards. But this exhibition had scarcely closed when the Rosenberg Gallery opened from 4th to 31st March to show a series of 28 recent works consisting of 20 canvases and 8 gouaches. This attracted enormous crowds. To avoid the results of success and the intruders who came after him,

Aztec face, the dreadful Garuda head only disgust ignorant and foolish people. If we feel horrified, our horror is sublimated by the mysticism or spirituality underlying them. We feel the presence of a myth, an epic or some supernatural fable behind the weird forms produced by the emotional violence of the tropical races. The Dragon of the Hesperides, the Dragon that embodies evil in Christian imagery, frighten nobody because they are fraught with all the prestige of the supernatural. The ogre in a fairy-tale by Perrault does not terrify children, because a Good Fairy thwarts all his evil designs. As for the disturbing images in dreams, they are usually only fleeting visions, poetic fictions, sports of the unconscious mind, and only rarely are they consistent plastic creations.

The *Seated Women* and *Reclining Women* by Picasso have, needless to say, none of the above attributes, they have neither religious feeling nor poetic idealism nor any literary pretext. The diagrammatic figures he had executed in 1927 were too unlike their models to shock or anger anyone. In those which he painted after 1937, however, we can still clearly recognize the person who served as a model, in spite of their monstrous deformities. It was not that he was anxious to preserve the resemblance, even though something of it remained in the picture. But nobody can deny that any of these 'Seated Women' are intended to be women, with all the physical

Picasso withdrew from the capital on the 25th of March and went to Juan-les-Pins, where he stayed for two months.

End of May—*On his return to Paris he used Lacourière's studio for engraving the thirty-one plates which were to serve as illustrations for Buffon's* Natural History—*thirty-one delightful aquatints which Sabartés says were executed "as his imagination moved him, but at least one every day". Other witnesses say that when they saw*

him at work, it was as though the animal he was portraying were standing before him, so vividly did every detail and every stroke combine to conjure up the expected form. As the book was not published by the time Vollard died, the task was completed by Fabiani and it appeared in 1942. Only 226 copies were printed, and it is now one of Picasso's most sought-after books, together with Ovid's Metamorphoses.

18th July 1936—*News now spread*

STILL-LIFE WITH RED BULL'S HEAD. PARIS, 26 FEBRUARY 1938. OIL AND RIPOLIN PAINT, 38¾″ × 52″. *Louise Leiris Gallery, Paris.*

of the serious disorders in Spain that were the beginning of the Civil War. The drama now developing decided Picasso, like many other artists at that time, to take a public stand on political questions. Already in 1908, *according to Maurice Raynal, when the socialist Francisco Ferrer was shot at Montjuich under Alfonso XIII, Picasso had felt the strongest resentment against "an act that would result in cruel upheavals in Spain". Picasso's choice was never in doubt:* he elected for the Republic. He was appointed Director of the Prado Museum by the Republican government and was to organize the evacuation and safe-keeping of the country's art-treasures. In 1937 when he denounced the bombing of the museum by General Franco's planes, it was in the belief that he had sided with justice that he said "At Valencia I saw the state of the pictures rescued from the Prado. The world must know that it was the

qualities of womanhood, and that they are seated. But the various organs of the woman have been dissociated and rearranged by the artist according to his own overweening though inexplicable requirements. In such a woman, who is taken to pieces and put together again by a jack-of-all-trades of genius, there is not really any metamorphosis as in other works by Picasso; there is a kind of interpretation or translation, an aesthetic reshaping. The greater that reshaping or renewal, the greater the distance between model and image will be, and the more upsetting the picture will be for the viewer. And it will disconcert all the more, in proportion as the apparent realism of intention has been the more vigorously asserted.

Whereas in his Cubist phase Picasso compressed his lyricism into abstract diagrams and confined his forms to geometrical figures, his inner tension increased in a sort of crescendo after *Guernica* and led him into an extreme form of naturalism. His worst onslaughts on the human figure were a sinister by-product or counterpart of his passion for truth. He wanted to paint truthfully, to be more truthful than nature. Everything goes to prove this: the powerful volumes, firm construction, brutal flood of light, the narrow space in which his figures are confined, which is usually a room roughly indicated by three walls and a ceiling. For us the whole layout of the visible world has become so fixed by our prejudices that we can no longer

Spanish people who saved Spanish art." Faced with the horror of war, he spoke up in angry defiance, using his genius to denounce the inhumanity of an event whose deeper meaning was only to become apparent some years later. In his efforts to help the martyred Spanish children Picasso sold many canvases that he had intended keeping, and several times sent large sums of money for that purpose. 1937—Picasso could not hide his contempt and hatred for the chief

apostle of the Spanish Right. He wrote a pamphlet (on 8th and 9th January) entitled Sueño y Mentira de Franco *(Dream and Lie of Franco). To illustrate this he engraved (between then and 7th June) eighteen etchings, touched with aquatint, of incredible violence. These engravings were also sold later in the form of postcards for the benefit of the Spanish Republican government. On 26th April, which was a market-day, the little Basque town of Guernica*

.JG WOMAN. 2 JULY 1937.
.JG AND AQUATINT, FIRST DRAFT, $27\frac{1}{4}'' \times 19\frac{3}{4}''$.

look through reality and see what is beyond it as Picasso's penetrating eye seems to do. We are so used to living surrounded by masks and disguises that we can no longer recognize the naked truth when we see it. In art, especially, what we take for true is false, and what we consider false is true. The truth is not always agreeable and consoling. If Pascal thought the human heart was foul, and if Baudelaire thought that anything natural is horrible, why should not Picasso portray a lovely little girl as a kind of monster, providing he sees her as such? The monster is there in front of my eyes, immodestly showing off its loathsome deformities. I look at it feeling both attracted and repelled, feeling within me the movements of flesh, viscera, the dense solid presence of something insistent and haunting, some strange thing which, however, is not unlike a woman wearing a bodice and a checked jacket—some relic of a disintegrated human world. After the trance I try to trace it in the crude reality of those lines and reliefs and colours which mean nothing but what they actually are. If they have no relation to a world of fantasy, can I dismiss this *Seated Woman* or *Woman Dressing Her Hair* as being mere monsters? The model has been mercilessly stripped of all its traditional values, so that the picture is less a free rendering of nature than a 'nature' of its own. It has nothing to do with the physiological order of things or with the tried and proven rules of optics,

was razed to the ground by planes marked with the swastika, which were then in Franco's service. Two thousand civilians lost their lives. The bombardment lasted three and a half hours and was intended to test the combined effects of explosive and incendiary bombs on a civilian population. Picasso, who had been asked by the Republican government in January 1937 for a large composition to decorate the Spanish pavilion at the International Exhibition in Paris, at once decided

to make this brutal act the theme of his work. On 1st May he drew a sketch containing all the essential features of the final version, though they are only roughly indicated. A whole month of work followed between this initial idea and the final picture. Christian Zervos has reproduced in the Cahiers d'Art (*13th year, Nos. 3–10, 1938) the photographs which Dora Maar took of* Guernica *in its various stages, as well as the sketches and drawings which either*

193

nor with the subjective concepts of ugliness or beauty. There is nothing here but the decisive intervention of a man who is indifferent both to the object's appearance and our idea of it—the intervention of an artist who is not interested in qualities but cares only for being itself.

Although Picasso's variations on the theme of the *Seated Woman* are very numerous, they avoid the monotony of device or of belonging to a series. Some of them are dominated by the curve, and have energetic modelling and a violent touch, while in others there is angular drawing, with geometrical volumes and tonal harmony. Sometimes the subject is so simplified, the form so abridged and the colour so limited that we see little more than a primitive mask on a pyramidal base (*Woman's Bust*, May 1943; *Woman in a Striped Bodice*, September 1943). With much the same outlook Picasso was also painting *Reclining Women*: in January 1939 a *Woman Lying on a Sofa*, shown before a window through which trees can be glimpsed; the *Reclining Nude* of September 1942, constructed according to Cubist principles, since it shows both front and back of the body; finally the astonishing *Reclining Nude and the Musician* (Musée d'Art Moderne, Paris), which is one of the most important works of the war period. Two figures are defined entirely by straight lines and curves, among a network of vertical, horizontal and diagonal lines all intersecting

accompanied the first beginnings or in some cases followed after the completion of the work. It can be seen that far from being an improvisation of genius, Guernica cost Picasso as much toil and care as it demanded his compassion and pity. The whole work was built up stage by stage, detail by detail, with drawings in black pencil, coloured crayons, pen and ink, and monochrome paintings and wash-drawings. During that immense work of preparation certain studies reached

such concentrated expressiveness that they became independent works of art: for instance, that painting of a horse's head with its haggard eyes, dilated nostrils, its tongue like the point of a dagger in its distended jaws, which is set against a background uniformly painted in black oil-paint. We must go back to 9th May to follow the work's entire development. An extremely detailed pencil-drawing shows that the artist first thought of his theme with a kind of blind excitement,

195

D WOMAN. 6 JANUARY 1937.
.0" × 32⅜". *Artist's Collection.*

at sharp angles. Though they are structurally unlike and their segments are differently assembled, they attract all the light in the picture, which is everywhere painted in subdued colours, spread over broad surfaces that together make an immense prism. The artist also used this spatial approach in a number of still-lifes, but these works all show signs of expressionism, though it is well not to generalize too much about this.

To do so would be to misunderstand an artist who delights in effacing his own tracks and following one excess by another, combining everything with its own opposite. The author of *Guernica* and the creator of so many freaks in 1937 engraved the *Portrait of Vollard* and the thirty-one plates for Buffon's *Natural History*, in which his exuberance was dazzlingly canalized along the ancient channels of classicism. As though with a smile on his lips, he painted with an easy brush birds in a cage (1937), fruits beside a pitcher, a fighting cock (1938), or, at night and by artificial light, objects that he handled with a more flexible technique but with a more serious touch, such as the *Still-life with Red Bull's Head* (1938). Here we see once more the bull of *Guernica* and the *Minotauromachia*. The candle was a new motif which Picasso began introducing into many of his still-lifes. In March 1940 at Royan he painted three still-lifes with fish (the *Conger-eels*; the *Soles*, in two versions); and a few landscapes,

and that under pressure of the moment he was unable to avoid a certain overstatement. When he began transferring this study to the canvas on 11th May in a calmer mood, there was already a tendency to simplify the drama and reduce it to the strictest possible limits. From that moment the right-hand section of Guernica *took on more or less the general appearance and structure now familiar to us. But the central and left sections were still to undergo important changes.*

Thus the dying horse, instead of rearing in that final protest seen in the finished work, completely collapsed with its head no more than an inanimate object crashing down to the ground; as for the dying warrior, who was at first more to the centre of the canvas, he lay with his face to the ground and one arm raised towards heaven. Finally, if, on the left, the mother clutching her son's dead body had almost reached the definitive stage, this was not the case with the bull,

196

FAUN UNVEILING A WOMAN. 12 JUNE 1936. AQUATINT, 12¾″ × 16¾″.

whose body was still obscured by the position of the lengthened head, which was turned away to the right. In the third phase the warrior was moved over to the left, while the sun against which he silhouetted his outstretched arm was given the form of an eye to which were later added, almost inevitably, the thin filaments of an electric bulb.

It was only in the fourth stage that the picture underwent two decisive changes that turned it into the work of vengeance with which we are all familiar. This is worth pondering over, for it was now that the drama, whittled down to its essentials and stripped of anything that might have dimmed it, was set in action. There are always two worlds facing each other, that which haunts the artist's mind, and the seething world of forms already alive on the canvas. The final work springs from this challenge and the countless exchanges between the two. Suddenly we see the horse's head lifted up to occupy a space in the centre of the canvas, with astonishing speed and ease, since at the same time, and in the very place where he could be prodigal of the joys of light and abandon himself to fresh emotional experiences, he was describing darkness and suffering in the immodest *Nude Dressing Her Hair* and the shocking *Women's Heads* which he painted on paper. Nor did he show any more tenderness towards children, as we see in *The Little Boy with a Lobster* (1941) or *The First Steps* (1943).

The series of freakish *Seated Women* continued into 1944, alternating with a series of portraits that were manneristic in their naturalism, and in fact almost prim, such as the *Portrait of Nush Eluard* (1941) and the *Portrait of Inès* (1942). Next to the elegant line and light tones with delicate modelling shown in these portraits, the *Seated Women* look carelessly executed with their heavy line, muddy pigments, drab or garish colours. The still-lifes of the war years were more carefully handled and show admirable strength and craftsmanship. Less lavish or decorative or logically arranged than those of 1925–26, they are quite as solid and well balanced and have more energy, more dramatic point and drive. The object placed before a window appears frequently as a theme. Short of a window, a looking-glass serves to throw out the light and give depth. The familiar guitar, jug and palette also reappear. The colour is more unified, the strokes and lines are smoother, the brush more abandoned, the

formerly occupied by the bull's body. The bull has turned its head round violently, changing position to take up the left side of the painting. In this new arrangement the artist had only to turn the warrior's head up towards the sky, leaving the dismembered body scattered over the ground (seventh version). There is an urge to say everything at once, yet also an absolute conciseness of language—two rules which the artist seems to have always had in mind. It is also significant that

the action, at first shown in the open air, was gradually moved into an enclosed space, since the final version shows a door on the right and wooden planks on the floor, quite apart from the electric light: all these features appeared not long before the work was completed.

As soon as it was finished Guernica *was installed in the Spanish pavilion. The picture thus gained world-wide recognition.* Guernica, *the outcry of a revolted soul demanding revenge, still*

DRAWING. JUAN-LES-PINS, 7 APRIL
INDIAN INK, 20″ ×

composition freer. Reminiscences of Cubism were becoming rarer and less noticeable, while the painter's lyricism overflowed with a strength that constantly threatened to destroy the forms that embodied it. What has always saved Picasso from the extravagance of the great expressionists is his intellectual clarity, his unfailing confidence as a draughtsman. Even when his most savage impulses might have broken up the contour to spread over the canvas, he was always warned in time by an infallible instinct for form. In expressing the most intense emotions and feelings such as anger, hatred, revolt and drama, it was never in the manner of a Soutine, a Marc, a Munch or a Kokoschka, but always as an artist incapable of sacrificing form to the ego. Painting, for him, is "an instrument of warlike aggression" and could never become a complaint, a whine, an ebbing of vitality, a nostalgic spiritual vagueness or the weak protest of the defeated.

The particular value of these still-lifes painted during and after the war lies in the outstanding energy of their conception and their no less impressive workmanship. The *Still-life with Ox-skull* (1942) and above all the superb *Still-life with Guitar* (1942) produce an immediate impact. In the latter work the table, the musical instrument, the plate glass and mirror are all rendered with incisive lines, sharply syncopated forms and pure bright colours. We admire the urgent but harmonious rhythm of this work, and the smooth strength of the contrasts, the way in which the soft curves of the table and guitar are balanced by the vertical line of the sword, firmly planted in the lower part of the composition. Another work of 1942, the *Still-life with Eggs*, is the only still-life in which Picasso made use of eggs in his plastic scheme, their elliptical shapes playing an essential part in relationship to the verticals, parallels, diagonals and the pattern of angles that combine to produce light and perspective. The skinned rabbit and dead chicken lying on the table would not have been enough to restore the balance, broken by the intersecting straight lines that start from entirely different angles of vision. It was by including the three eggs and giving them light, that the painter found the solution to his problem. From 1943 onwards Picasso enjoyed painting flowers in vases, baskets of fruit and ears of corn, according to the discouragement or hope he felt during the

serves as a witness today and has lost nothing of its power.

Early in 1937 Picasso hired a studio in the rue des Grands-Augustins so as to be able to work undisturbed and in better conditions. Known as the 'Barrault loft' because it was formerly occupied by the actor Jean-Louis Barrault, this studio—which Picasso still uses—soon became famous. Guernica was one of the first canvases to be painted there.

The storm unleashed by the Spanish

war had not yet nearly died down. For Picasso this resulted also in the series of Weeping Women *of 1938. To this sequence belongs the etching with aquatint which is reproduced on page 190. Then he made many portraits of Mlle Dora Maar, his new companion. In painting these he invented and used for the first time his own convention of combining the profile with the front view of the face. Let us turn back to the early months of 1939, or more exactly to 17th January, which was*

Occupation. With the rationing of electricity and food, the Occupation gave him fresh themes such as the lighted candle, the coffee-pot, tomato-plants, leeks, a chicken prepared for cooking. No artist ever had a firmer grasp on reality, or ever portrayed it enhanced with so much meaning that normally escapes us, and with all the sensations such meanings give him. Always aware of the external world, he puts into his work only what he has seen for himself, sick people and acrobats, musicians and dancers, the bull from the Spanish ring, women he has loved, or his children, his furniture. At Dinard and Royan he naturally painted fish. As for the 'Catalan' Side-board (1943) he looked at it for months at the 'Catalan' restaurant in the rue des Grands-Augustins. He had the tomato-plant in his room— the Parisian housewives were then growing vegetables on their balconies to eke out the rations. The 1920 landscapes were brought back from Juan-les-Pins, as he had brought back his first Cubist canvases from Horta de Ebro. The dazzling seascapes of 1940 were made at Royan, and the Paris of the Liberation inspired his most moving landscapes, just as ten years later Vallauris suggested the little cottages peeping through greenery and flowers.

Picasso is always in direct contact with life. When his works seem to be thought out in an abstract way or entirely imaginary there is

varnishing-day for the last exhibition Picasso gave before the war. It was held in the Rosenberg Gallery and was full of surprises. It contained thirty-three still-lifes, all exceptionally gentle, most of them painted while he was still engaged on Guernica. Almost a narrative of his private life, as Jaime Sabartés has pointed out in Portraits and Memories, these canvases contained all the everyday things with which Picasso likes to surround himself.

'Picasso: Forty Years of His Art' was the title given to the important retrospective show held in New York in 1939 under the auspices of the Museum of Modern Art (N.Y.) and the Art Institute of Chicago. It consisted of 364 paintings, sculptures, water-colours, drawings and engravings. This exhibition finally established the artist's fame in the United States.

After spending the summer of 1939 at Antibes, Picasso returned to Paris

THE POET JAIME SABARTÉS. ROYAN, 22 OCTOBER 1939. OIL, 18⅜″ × 15¼″. *Private Collection, Paris.*

generally some link, however slender, that gives them a firm connection with reality—some person or object, animal or vegetable, or some emotion they gave him, whether joy or suffering, irritation or pity, love or hatred. He seeks his inspiration neither in history nor fiction, nor in books nor museums (except satirically), but in existence itself, in the finite, the contingent. He did not discover the bull through reading Greek mythology, and if the animal later became the Minotaur, yet the *corrida* underlay its changing forms. Nor were his still-lifes ever influenced by some purple passage from Colette or a Dutch painting. He cared little about rendering appearances. Cosmology means nothing to him. He is less intent on observing the object than in, so to speak, entering it, informing it, seeing the world from the object's point of view. There is nothing arbitrary and nothing created *in abstracto* in Picasso's work, however much we might think so. The key ideas of his work are a natural order and the assertion of an individual mind. The things he examines, dissects, contracts, distends or undoes try to protest, they sometimes grate or jam or creak. But in spite of everything there is enough in

WOMAN LEANING ON HER ELBOWS,
READING. PENCIL DRAWING, $10\frac{5}{8}'' \times 8\frac{3}{8}''$.

CAFÉ AT ROYAN. ROYAN, 15 AUGUST 1940. OIL AND RIPOLIN PAINT, 38¾″ × 52″. *Artist's Collection.*

for a few days at the end of August. With the declaration of war impending he decided to retire to Royan, where he arrived on 1st September. He spent the rest of the year there, as well as the first eight months of 1940. This stay was not so calm as might appear, as Picasso returned to Paris on five occasions, staying only a few days each time, except for two months there (15th March to 16th May) during the tragic spring of 1940. At the time of the fall of France many of his

friends advised him to go to America or Mexico, but Picasso refused to leave France, and on 24th August he returned to Paris and remained there for the rest of the war period.

1941–44—During those tragic years which put an end to all that normally makes up the pleasure of existence, Picasso could hardly remain aloof from the universal drama. He who had painted Guernica was not likely to reflect the war like a photographer; but as he said himself, "Perhaps the

common between him and them for some compromise to be reached, even though it remains insecure.

One feels a mixture of admiration and fear while watching this intrepid man shaping, constructing, trying to extract every possible potentiality from matter; superimposing his own world on to the real world, moulding it in his hands, giving line, volume and density to the crude *magma*; making direct attacks on inertia, shapelessness and heaviness, in other words on evil itself, yet finding no issue to his harassing search and no reward for his self-imposed torment. Picasso once said, "For me, art is a search for salvation." But we may doubt whether his wish will ever be granted. What we may be sure of is that no artist has greater power than he for transfiguring the world through his own resources, for conquering it and wresting its secrets and making it his obedient slave. But nobody is more aware than he of its absolute stability, its enduring sameness. He has penetrated the world through and through in search of his own ego, with the buoyancy of a conqueror and all the fury of a baffled despot. This man who wants peace for others refuses it for himself. When his adventure takes him too far and he feels himself carried away he swings the wheel and returns to dry land. It is then that he enters most deeply into reality, and begins a new phase of activity. He takes up sculpture again.

historians will notice that my style changed during the war." A theme that obsessed him during those years was the Seated Woman, *in which he redistributed facial features at the dictate of his emotions, achieving a sombre, agonizing cruelty which suggests better than any description could do, the intolerable atmosphere of those days.*

At the same time as these 'portraits' he made a sequence of still-lifes in which certain objects occur more often than others, being obviously chosen for their topical meaning, such as the lighted candle used to offset the restrictions on electricity; the tomato-plant he had in his own flat; while the skinned rabbit, the leeks and the morbid ox-skull — of which the original can be seen in the rue des Grands-Augustins studio — were also his own.

It was while waiting to return home — for he was then sharing his time between the studio, where he worked at

In the same year as his expressionistic 'trance' led him to compose *Guernica*, he seems to have tried to find his inner balance by carving on pebbles, as did our remote ancestors. At the height of his Baroque style in painting, he carved pieces of bone, like primitive man, or started cutting out, joining together and colouring strips of cardboard with a boyish enthusiasm. Whereas the painter had passed beyond realism, the sculptor was approaching matter in the raw, limiting his own intervention to a minimum and assembling the most unlike objects, blending the least compatible materials, exploiting the most unexpected and trivial things which seem at the opposite pole from plastic art. He took a child's scooter and fixed it on a metal stalk, added a bird's feather, and the result was a wader. Two bits of wire and a chunk of wood covered with plaster were enough to make a bird: a bicycle saddle and a pair of handlebars became a bull's head. Using whatever bits of discard he could lay hands on, Picasso used them for non-functional purposes. Without in the least changing or deforming them a single gesture was enough for him to put them together in some unexpected way and thus

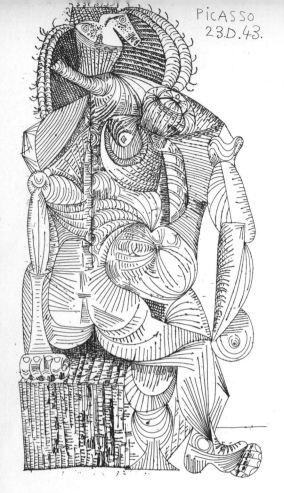

SEATED WOMAN. 23 DECEMBER 1943. ETCHING
(9¾″ × 5¼″) FOR 'CONTRÉE', BY DESNOS.

night, and his flat in the rue La Boétie—that Picasso began writing, both to kill time and to avenge himself for the privations imposed by the Germans, a one-act burlesque play called Desire Trapped by the Tail. This was finished on 17th January 1941 and was performed in March 1944 to a large gathering at the Leiris's flat, with Louise and Michel Leiris, Dora Maar, Simone de Beauvoir, Albert Camus, Raymond Queneau and Jean-Paul Sartre taking parts.

Picasso was not yet a Communist, but with Paris occupied by the Nazis we can understand what was in the minds of those who announced that he was. At the same time there were others who began spreading rumours that he was half Jewish, through his mother. After pointing to him for years as one of the masters of 'degenerate art' the Nazis did not hesitate to approach him in the hope of persuading him to collaborate. They failed miserably, but did not dare to touch him and were satisfied with refusing permission to show his pictures. Picasso would not compromise with Vichy any more than with Berlin. As a result the most absurd and vitriolic attacks were made on him, and there were even journalists who tried to popularize slogans such as "Matisse in the dustbin" or "Certify Picasso" and pass them off for aesthetic judgments. During that time his oldest friend Max Jacob died in the concentration camp at Drancy,

RECLINING WOMAN. PARIS,
PENCIL, 8⅖″ ×

transfer them from the sphere of the concrete into that of art. These things became authentic 'sculptures', absolutely original, obvious and undeniable. He made masks, animals' heads and amusing silhouettes with matches and paper. He continued modelling and casting figurines, busts and human skulls in bronze. He did all this during the war when his pictures showed no sign of any sculptural features. But after 1944 his painting and sculpture appear to have come together again. It was in 1944 that he made one of his most important and largest pieces, *The Man with a Lamb*, which is 7 feet 4 inches high. His feverish activity spread out into every direction, into every artistic medium: painting, sculpture, ceramics, which he now took up, engraving, which he had neglected since 1938, and lithography to which he now gave much of his time.

The 1944 Autumn *Salon* marked the beginning of this exceptionally fruitful period. The liberation of Paris (24th August) filled him with new emotion and he left his surly isolation. He felt the need for living on more friendly terms with his contemporaries, for sharing their happiness and hopes and their will to begin a fresh life. He agreed to take part in the *Salon* for the first time. At the Autumn *Salon* he exhibited seventy-four pictures and five sculptures which firmly established his fame. Foreign countries honoured him and

organized exhibitions of his works. When he could have relaxed his efforts and lived a quiet life and looked back proudly on his career, he set to work again even more energetically than before. He was still painting views of Paris in a style which, as might be expected, had nothing derivative about it. If we compare *The Square du Vert-Galant* (1943) and its tropical exuberance with those landscapes full of jarring lines and gloomy colours of 1945 we are at once struck by a change of tone. We might ask what was the meaning of those views of Paris, in which the bridges and quays of the Seine, Notre-Dame, the Panthéon, the Eiffel Tower and the Champs-Élysées all crowd into the same canvas, together with bits of houses full of windows. Why such a jumble of architecture, such a prismatic composition? Why so much pathos, when we are told that Picasso was trying to pay homage to the recently freed and revived capital? It was because his heart and his sensitiveness were still bruised by the effects of the war. The days of calm and relief were still fewer than those of tension and torment. The death's head which he set beside a bunch of leeks, in defiance of logic or necessity, or next to a lamp or jug, points to a deep-seated pessimism. But as soon as he removed the skull from his still-lifes they had a remarkable freshness. One of them, to which we draw attention, is perhaps the simplest

THE OSTRICH. 1937. AQUATINT, 10⅝″ × 8¾″.
ILLUSTRATION FOR BUFFON'S 'NATURAL HISTC
(Fabiani, 1942).

THE COCK. 1937. AQUATINT, $11\frac{1}{4}'' \times 9\frac{1}{4}''$. ILLUSTRATION FOR
BUFFON'S 'NATURAL HISTORY' (Fabiani, 1942).

and with one or two others Picasso insisted on attending his funeral and paying his last respects.

25th August 1944—The nightmare ended and Paris was set free. The committee of the *Autumn* Salon, which was to open six weeks after the Liberation, offered Picasso a whole room to himself. He accepted this mark of sympathy and showed seventy-four paintings and five sculptures. This was the first time he had ever exhibited in a Salon. This event had an exceptional and symbolic importance, for at the same time as an official tribute was being paid to a man whose attitude during the war had been above reproach, the public wanted to honour an artist whose work, after being the target for the grossest attacks and insults, had now become a symbol of liberty. On 8th October extremists created scenes by tearing the canvases down from the walls and demanding either their money back or some form of explanation. Picasso's declaration of official adherence to the French Communist Party on the 5th October

212

and most expressive still-life ever painted. This *Still-life with Enamelled Pan* (1945) was painted in one night. As he was disturbed during the day by both friends and busybodies, it was in the quiet and peace of the night hours that Picasso refound his inspiration and his unspoilt capacity for work. He enjoyed the melancholy of those shapeless hours, he shared in the conflict between the artificial light and the shadows, the fantastic changing forms thinning out or looming upwards, enlarging and contracting according to the placing of the light and the moving of this or that object.

There is nothing but a lighted candle, a jug and a pan set on the table. The composition would collapse if anything were removed. The yellow of the candlestick and the blue of the enamel pan oppose their heavy lustre to the neutrals, the brown of the table and the grey of the jug and background. The artist has not tried to render the natural or artificial light as would Caravaggio, Honthorst or Georges de La Tour. The light here is invented, transcribed with a few stretches of colour, lines and shapes. The flame is in the shape

HUMAN SKULL. PARIS, 1943.
BRONZE. HEIGHT, $11\frac{5}{8}''$.

of a white spear-head, the shadow a black, sideways cone. They are forms which portray what is least definable and tangible in reality, forms which define the volume and internal structure of things simultaneously. By a freely interpreted echo of Cubism these things can be seen in the sum of all their parts. Everything in this canvas is real and imagined, in the sense that while we can easily recognize the things Picasso wanted to represent, yet not one of them is the same as its material model, either in contour, relief or proportions. Picasso has re-created their essence, their permanence and truth by lending them his own strong individuality. Nobody could deny that this candlestick, pan and jug are in a sense more solid and more concrete, more convincingly present both in themselves and to our eyes than their originals. He drew them with such a firm, deft stroke, and their measurements and colours are so precisely worked out in relation to each other, the work is so perfectly balanced that it would have a kind of classical perfection, were it not that a certain line has been given a cruel twist, or if this or that colour had not an almost toxic quality, and if the style itself did not stress the shameless devices of an eccentric, surgical touch. But any museum-picture would look completely dead next to such oddness and contradiction, such liberties which have been unified by logic.

might have had something to do with these scenes.

1945—The first six months of this year witnessed the return to France of those who had survived the concentration camps. The whole country was shaken by the magnitude of the drama. Picasso then decided to record something that words cannot describe and began one of the greatest canvases he painted after Guernica. *The* Charnel-house *is a kind of "Grief-less Pietà, an Entombment without*

mourners, a Requiem without pomp", as it was correctly described by Alfred Barr in his book, Picasso, Fifty Years of his Art, New York, 1946. *For the first time since the war, Picasso left the capital to spend his vacation on the Côte d'Azur in August 1944. The time was approaching when he was to spend most of his year in the south. He was in Paris again in early November, and on 2nd November he made his first visit to the workshop of the Mourlot*

PORTRAIT OF MAYA, AGED 8. PARIS, 29 AUGUST 1943. PENCIL.

THE 'SQUARE DU VERT-GALANT'. PARIS, 25 JUNE 1943. OIL, 26″ × 36¾″. *Artist's Collection.*

brothers in the rue de Chabrol. Nobody knew, that day, that he was embarking on one of his most extraordinary undertakings. It is now apparent that on that day Picasso had already decided to return to lithography, a process which he had left untouched since 1930, otherwise he would not have taken with him three 'women's heads' cut out in paper, which he wanted to have transferred to the block, on the spot, by the best pressman in the workshop. He did not know, however, that for the next four months he would be returning to that shop day after day to toil like a work-

man, arriving at nine in the morning and only leaving his work late in the evening, often after eight o'clock. He was liked by the workmen who at once recognized him as one of themselves by his love of work and his doggedness. He completely changed the whole atmosphere of the workshop by his presence. Fernand Mourlot has let it be known that Picasso used only his own tools, consisting of no more than a little penknife which served as a scraper, while for graving-tool he had something that looked like a sickle, which he had made himself. There was no limit to his inventiveness during

In 1945 Picasso returned to the Côte d'Azur for the first time since the war. New themes began to appear in his canvases, such as fish, cuttle-fish, sea-urchins, lemons, leafage and flowers in a vase. The next year, the extraordinary rumour came to Paris that Picasso was decorating the walls of the Antibes Museum in the Grimaldi Palace. So far he had never tried monumental painting. His friends had never even heard him mention it. But on the 8th of September he had remarked to M. de la Souchère, the curator of the museum, "I've always wanted to paint big surfaces, but I've never been given any." He was given some. He set to work at once in a large room in the Grimaldi Palace which he transformed into a studio. Night and day, with incredible enthusiasm, glowing with inspiration, his bewitched hands conjured up a world of centaurs, fauns, satyrs and the huge still-lifes which were soon to fill the 'Picasso Museum' and attract a stream of visitors from all over the world. These visitors were stupefied by what they saw, because they failed to understand these pastorals and idylls which revive the ideal of a race of creatures endowed with happiness, innocence and harmony. The nightmare of *Guernica*, the massacres of the bull-ring, the disfigured 'seated women' were now forgotten. There were no more bloodthirsty monsters, no more avenging Furies or gods of punishment and remorse. The Minotaur gave way to Io transformed into a heifer, and Nemesis fled before the gentle Amaryllis. The shepherds learnt

.L-LIFE WITH SEA-URCHINS. ANTIBES, 1946.
CONTÉ, 20⅜" × 26⅜".

the poetic warbling of the flute from the singing birds, while the little horned gods danced round them. Picasso gave the title 'Joie de vivre' to the pastoral, painted on fibro-cement and ten feet square, which covers a whole wall in the Grimaldi Palace. The title is significant. Three other panels, 8 feet 4 inches high, portray in a graphic rather than a pictural style a satyr blowing through his reed pipes, a young woman leaping into the air, a centaur with a trident in his hand. Near by we can admire an immense still-life, also on fibro-cement, which is dryly drawn and very sober in colour, showing a fish, a ewer and a bowl of fruit. In another room, but this time painted on plywood, is a still-life with a knife, a glass and some sliced fruit. Farther on there are some sea-urchins, a bottle and three apples, then a dish of grapes, a guitar and two apples on a plate. These unusually large still-lifes are followed by others of normal size, more freely painted on canvas, altogether less stiff and painted with a full impasto: a cuttle-fish waving its tentacles, an octopus and a lamprey with their curves all interwoven, a golden-yellow lemon next to a purplish aubergine, some flatfish and sea-urchins with their bristling black-tipped quills. The Antibes Museum also has paintings of fishermen and fishmongers, a kneeling goat, and a reminiscence of an earlier theme in two great *Reclining Women*, straightforward in volumes but monumentally constructed. Lastly, there is

THE OWL. ANTIBES, 8 NOVEMBER 1946.
LEAD-PENCIL, 26″ × 20″.

the tremendous panel representing *Ulysses and the Sirens,* which is flooded with sunshine.

What is the meaning of all these images of the pleasures of everyday life? How did he come to paint these eclogues which all radiate such grace and simple happiness? Their purity of line, subtle colouring, their bucolic themes set against horizons of sea and sky, remind us of Theocritus, a Theocritus who has exchanged the flute for the brush. Of course this was not the first time that Picasso sought his themes in antiquity. In 1920 he had already drawn centaurs, and in 1930 he engraved Ovid's *Metamorphoses.* In 1932 he painted Daphnis playing the pipes beside a drowsing Chloe, and in 1934 he illustrated the *Lysistrata* of Aristophanes. But that antiquity belonged to school books, fifth-century Greek vases, Winckelmann and the art-historians, whereas the ancient world portrayed on the walls of Antibes Museum has nothing to do with its origins, except through the subjects he exploits. Even the Greeks had never known how to portray with such power and ease the musical revels and divine *far niente* of their nymphs and shepherds, however much they respected human anatomy in their limning of the gods and always viewed nature with a calm, objective eye. The rustic deities that Picasso brought from Thrace and Boeotia were transformed in his hands.

those months, when there was nothing to hinder his freedom and genius. Far from keeping to the rules and traditions of the craft—which he mastered in a few minutes—as usual he wanted to try his hand at what had never been done before. He gave himself manual jobs to do that any ordinary craftsman would have recoiled from, but his successes were equal to his daring. Working without any fixed programme, during those four months he cut more than thirty plates, some of them in colour, which the Louise Leiris Gallery was to publish with the rest of his later lithographs. At the end of the winter Picasso returned to this work, but this time in his studio, rue des Grands-Augustins, using zinc blocks in preference to stone as being easier to handle—though lithographers generally find working in zinc more difficult as well as less pleasant.

Thanks to the invaluable catalogue drawn up by Fernand Mourlot (Picasso: Lithographer, 2 vols., 1949–50, with a Preface by Sabartés) we can count 179 lithographic works produced between 2nd November 1945 and 30th May 1949. The figure has been almost doubled since then. They include all the themes most dear to the artist, still-lifes, corrida scenes, fauns with pipes, centaurs, free interpretations of famous works (such as David and Bathsheba, after Cranach), young women's heads. Among the latter, dated 14th June 1946, are ten lithographs of an admirable purity of

THE MAN WITH A LAMB. PARIS, 1944. BRONZE, 7 FT 4 IN. HIGH.

line, depicting the features of Françoise Gilot, a young woman whom he had recently met and who became his

221

TAURS ON THE SEA-SHORE. IBES, 1946. 20⅜″ × 26⅜″.

THE FLOWER-TRIMMED HAT. 10 APRIL 1940. OIL, $28\frac{3}{4}'' \times 24''$. *Private Collection, Paris.*

companion. *This survey of his litho-graphical works would be incomplete without mention of the series of animals which make him one of the finest animal artists of our age: the owl, the*

toad, the lobster, the chicken, not to mention the pigeon and dove.
1946—*After a short voyage to Golfe-Juan and Antibes in April, Picasso returned to his rue des Grands-*

DEATH'S HEAD AND LEEKS. PARIS, 18 MARCH
OIL, $35\frac{5}{8}'' \times 52''$. *Louise Leiris Gallery,*

They assumed the shape of his dreams and fantasies. They dance and leap and twirl in an ecstasy which is heightened by the instinctive awareness that nothing endures. Their bodies are remarkably lengthened and narrowed, obeying that alternate contraction and expansion imposed by the state of Picasso's conscience or mood.

But we must try to explain why he produced these faunish visions, these rustic idylls, this escape into a pagan Eden. How can we explain this generous impulse, such a spring-like renewal of life that gives these Antibes works their exceptional tonic quality? Perhaps it was because Picasso, who loved the Mediterranean and had always felt its appeal, had now come into close contact with the regions where man first found his human stature, the shores which brought life to the oldest themes of human history. He had just met the woman who was to become his close companion and the mother of

his last two children. He was finding new friendly faces everywhere; he had found new reasons for continuing his struggle to advance still farther along a road he had thought already closed to his tireless pursuit. He had discovered the happiness of having vast surfaces on which to paint, difficulties to overcome which no one else could have even got round, especially those panels of cement that dismayed the eye and the painter's brush. Everything combined to inspire him, mythology and nature, the people and objects of everyday life. Everything seemed to bring him happiness. The portraits of Françoise Gilot have a Madonna-like appearance, in contrast to the tormented figures he was painting a few years earlier. The *Seated Women* he painted in Paris during that winter were treated very like the nymphs in the Antibes pastorals. Though he now had as much canvas as he wanted, he continued to use plywood. The Mediterranean influence was still at work. But for how long? He is so made that every pleasure seems to conceal some kind of pitfall, every delight has only a deceptive gloss. Experiments are hardly finished when he begins to question their validity and implications. He is only too well aware that life is not a constant happiness. So his searching eye found darkness as well as light, the suffering that lurks beneath a smile, the fear that lies behind every desire. The *Lobster on a Table* (December 1946) and even more *The Cock and Knife* (March 1947) radiate an

Augustins studio, where he passed the months of May and June. In July he left the capital for Ménerbes, where we know from one of his drawings that he was still staying in August. From there he went to the Côte d'Azur, sharing his time between Golfe-Juan and Antibes. It was then that he began spending his time in the Grimaldi Palace. By some miracle which those who witnessed it are at a loss to explain, he transformed it into one of those places in which one would

be glad to spend the rest of one's life, for that is what the Antibes Museum seems to suggest. The facts of the matter are worth recording, however briefly. On 8th September 1946, M. Dor de la Souchère, the curator of the museum, was with Picasso on the beach at Golfe-Juan when the artist voiced his regret at never having been given large surfaces to paint. It might be asked whether regret was the proper word. The 'regret' was perhaps no more than a vague desire, and no

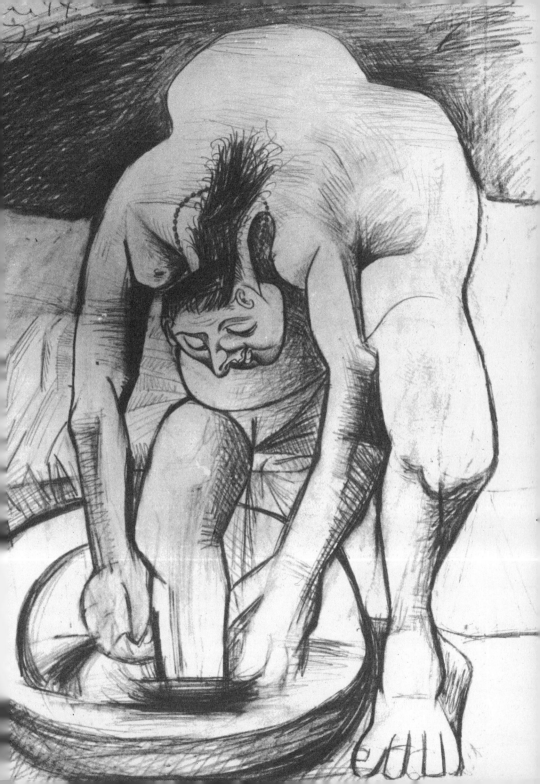

WOMAN SEATED IN AN ARM-CHAIR. 5 MARCH 1953. OIL ON PLYWOOD, 40″ × 32⅜″. *Louise Leiris Gallery, Pa*

COCK AND KNIFE. 21 MARCH 1947. OIL, 29¼" × 36¾". *Mr. and Mrs. W. Ganz Collection, New York.*

sooner was it formulated than its fulfilment became probable. It remains to be explained how a chance meeting on a beach could result in such a museum as the one at Antibes, which is an absolutely new and unique achievement. "Surfaces? You want big surfaces? I can offer you some." The very next day M. de la Souchère gave Picasso a free hand in one of the museum rooms. Using it as a studio, the artist started work there and came every day for over

four months, arriving shortly after noon and leaving only at nightfall. As canvas was hard to find at that time, M. de la Souchère got together all the materials he could find in the shops at Antibes, such as sheets of fibro-cement and plywood, and had them brought to the museum. It is doubtful whether any painter was ever gripped by such a fever as, happily, now filled Picasso. With his usual speed and shrewdness he grasped all the essential features of

227

intense dramatic feeling that springs from the artist's affection for animals. But his favourite theme at that time was the owl, which appeared for the first time in one of the Antibes Museum paintings. No doubt he was aware of the strange chance that brought him 'Minerva's bird' at a time when he was living in an atmosphere of myth. We can imagine the poetic associations he must have made between his private thoughts and those fables in which the owl is the familiar of witches. In any case the bird, which Picasso kept in his studio, so that it shared his nocturnal hours and never allowed him to forget its presence, gradually became an obsession. Either in its cage or perched on a branch or on the back of a chair, this owl figured in most of his paintings, drawings and engravings and, as we shall see, in many of his sculptures and pots. This wounded owl, that was picked up in a lane in Antibes one autumn night and given to the artist, became in his work a kind of essence of owlness, for him the only real, authentic Owl. When the bird died two years later its double continued to exist and multiply in his canvases, on paper, in plaster, bronze and clay, very much alive not only in these reincarnations but sometimes even in the human faces and figures

PAN. VALLAURIS, 10 MARCH 1948.
LITHOGRAPH, 26″ × 20⅜″.

he portrayed. The triangular volume he used to represent the owl's body, and his way of rendering the glint of the round eyes by two circles inside an oval, are often found in his drawings of people. Whatever meaning or appearance he gave the owl, and he certainly gave it hundreds of different ones, Picasso repeated this theme long after he found fresh symbols in new experiences.

He returned to the Midi early in the summer of 1947. Passing through a village where pottery has been made for two thousand years, he was fascinated by the work of the Provençal artisans, who with a simple turn of the hand could transform a crude lump of clay into a wonderful variety of forms and colours. He could not resist the temptation to become a potter. He quickly picked up the traditional skills of the craft, and found that since early times they had remained subject to unvariable laws. If he found it impossible to break these laws, yet he gave this art, to which he was a stranger, a new lease of life, a life of his own which he gave out without stint or calculation, with a passionate curiosity that had only increased with age. He sat down at the wheel, kneaded the clay, then shaped jugs, vases, dishes, plates, figurines; painted and glazed or varnished them, and put them in the kiln, using all his resources of intuition,

PAUL LANGEVIN. 1946.
INK-DRAWING.

virtuosity and imagination. The range of his decorative schemes was drawn from all that he had already observed or discovered—the story of the Minotaur, Greek eclogues, the arena, fishing scenes, all the living things of earth and sea. Under the pressure of his thumb a vase would assume the shape of a woman, or a dove, a vulture, a goat, an owl, a marrow. His statuettes of human figures echo the terra-cotta idols of the Aegean or of Cyprus. Like the ancient Peruvian potters he made vessels which were at the same time effigies of animals or human beings. He rehandled all the ancient forms, brought old formulas up to date and upset all the conventional terms of the craft, exploiting them for his own unexpected ends. His hands made Baroque vases, but also vases of classical purity, and set classical patterns on Baroque forms or Baroque decoration on classical forms. Picasso did not give up pottery. But the painter and sculptor continued their collaboration, though unfortunately without profit for the rest of mankind. It was hoped that the models he created at Vallauris would be reproduced in large numbers and thus reach the masses, to brighten up the existence of ordinary people and refine their sensibility and taste. Was the cost of mass-production too high? Or were the utilitarian qualities of these prototypes thought to be unworthy of their aesthetic qualities? What happened was that Picasso's pots became show-pieces and

THE SCREECH-OWL. 1950.
BRONZE, 14⅜″ HIGH.

articles of luxury, unique pieces which were sold to flatter the vanity of the middle classes and fill the purses of tradesmen. Picasso certainly did not intend his efforts and sacrifices to be nothing more than an exercise of 'pure' art, or a dead-end experiment. That is why, although his ceramics are of great significance, it is above all in relation to Picasso himself and because of the place they occupy in his work. There is no doubt that in turning his hand to this technique he at once enlarged his own field of invention and gave a further stimulus to his imagination, that most precious of all gifts which in his case is so lively, so profound, yet always liable to restlessness and doubt. While being aware of his fertility, we can hardly admit that these thousands of pieces of pottery he made at Vallauris did nothing to hold up his activities in painting, sculpting and engraving.

His son Claude was born in 1947. Picasso was touched, and enjoyed depicting the child. This new theme also gave him new means of expression. On plywood, he painted the little Claude either alone in his cradle or in an arm-chair, or in his mother's arms. Later, he painted him in a play-pen, waving toys. The lines move gracefully, festooning and embroidering all kinds of graphic variations round the young figure, the metal struts of the play-pen describing a sort of fugue. One version of this is particularly

the landscape, as well as the land's secret history and that of its people, and started creating works of such mysterious transparency that they are an integral part of the setting for which they were made and in which they were born. The secret of the Antibes Museum might also be sought in the admission he once made to his friend Sabartés: "I did what I could there, and did it with pleasure, because for once I had the feeling that I was working for the mass of man."

1947—Returning to Paris in mid-January, he remained there until the beginning of August, when he went back to Golfe-Juan. The south now seemed to contain some special inspiration for him and to play an indirect part in the prodigious revival we have seen in his work since the war. News no less surprising than that of the previous year reached Paris early in the autumn: Picasso had become a potter. He had taken up ceramics while staying at Vallauris.

232

9   7.11.45

1948—*For a whole year, until October 1948, he went to work every afternoon at the 'Madoura' pottery belonging to Suzanne and Georges Ramié, where he picked up the secrets of a craft about which he previously knew nothing. The 149 pieces which were on show at the Maison de la* Pensée Française (rue de l'Élysée) *from November 1948 to January 1949 amounted to hardly a tenth of his output. In fact, in that one year he produced some 2,000 pieces. Horned heads, Jupiter-like faces, suns and moons, men and women playing flutes, fishermen, nymphs and centaurs, owls and bulls, dancing-girls with heaving breasts and their hips like rounded vases—he brought a whole race of people into being, made us familiar with them by labouring day after day in an endless, daring improvisation that involved discoveries of form, design, colour and material. Vallauris quickly became world-famous and attracted a stream of visitors which changed the whole life of the little old village. It was thus a gesture of understandable gratitude when in February 1950 the local Town Council unanimously made Picasso a Freeman of their community. To seal this pact, Picasso gave the commune a replica of* The Man with a Lamb, *which was installed in the market-place.*

1949–51—*At the same time as his work in ceramics, Picasso carried on his painting and sculpting. The birth of his son Claude in 1947 (this was his third child), then of his daughter Paloma in 1949 explains the large number of 'Maternities' in which we see the children with their mother, Françoise Gilot. He also painted them separately, catching from day to day their postures and games, their happy or anxious expressions. These*

WOMAN. PARIS, 1943.
BRONZE, 72″ HIGH.

appealing with the baby lying down and a skein of wool unwound and criss-crossed round the fanciful outlines of the pen. All the father's intimate tenderness comes to the surface in such a work. Or we see the little boy in his chair or pram, or playing with a wooden horse. After 1950 he is no longer seen alone, but accompanied by his sister Paloma, who had just recently been born. Picasso then began a series of childhood scenes which are full of charm without being sentimental, and in which the chastest of emotions is, paradoxically, rendered through an obviously expressionistic technique. As the two children developed, the pictures became more frequent. We see them at their games, outings or meals, and sometimes asleep. We sense that Picasso was trying to avoid glib effects and to exclude sentimentality. Thus he used a deliberately clumsy line, spontaneous, workmanlike but deliberately careless, with thick, casual colours and loosely proportioned forms. He disfigured and disjointed those who were most dear to him, made them submit to all sorts of deformities and streaked their faces with brutal strokes of line and colour. In spite of that they have the freshness and innocence of their childhood and are not without signs of paternal affection. It is hard to explain how Picasso was able to express the finer human emotions while at the same time violating the natural order and using a language so unsuitable to his subject. There are plenty of touching details such

works are full of tenderness, as are the numerous landscapes he made at Vallauris, showing the south as it is known only to few, the black, gaunt Midi of the long winter days.

As for Picasso's sculpture, its reputation dates from that period. We had to await the publication of Kahnweiler's book, The Sculptures of Picasso (1949), *before this aspect of his activities was properly recognized. This is all the more surprising as sculpture had always been one of the*

artist's main preoccupations, the first of his pieces in this medium dating from 1899. It is quite true that before the recent war the public never had any opportunity of seeing Picasso's sculptures, apart from the two plaster Women's Heads *which were shown in the Spanish pavilion at the International Exhibition in 1937. On the other hand, after the war, apart from the* Autumn (Liberation) Salon, *which showed the notorious* Bull's Head *made out of a saddle and*

as the hair-ribbon, the little hands clasped on an apron, a cheek as round as the ball the child is holding, a little girl's face the image of her doll's. As the years went by the brother and sister took on childishly grave expressions. *The Luncheon* (1953) shows them at table, watched over by their mother with her sweeping protective gesture. The drawing is simplified, the form better defined and the composition more studied than before. Volume and space are no longer obtained by means of values or touches merging into each other, but entirely by very marked lines and flat patches of red, blue and green (page 243). In later pictures we see Claude and Paloma writing or drawing, bending gracefully over their task. Picasso's manner was again modified. For instance, he returned to a device he had used before in his *Papiers collés* and in a series of paintings of 1928—the dissociation of form and colour.

Of course the theme of family life was not the only one he was handling. But it is not always easy to grasp the cause or motive for some of his exploits, apart from his desire to be constantly renewing himself and that inner fire which enables him to live without being consumed. We might ask, for example, what was the origin of the daring research to be noticed in the two versions of *The Kitchen*, dated November 1948. What was his aim in making these two monochrome compositions, which the untutored eye might regard

handlebars, we should recall the various exhibitions which were held either at the Maison de la Pensée Française (November 1948: The Man with a Lamb; November 1950: a retrospective show of about fifty bronzes), or at the Leiris Gallery (October 1948 and May–June 1953), or at the May Salon of 1952: The Goat. Applying to sculpture the same principles as in the Papier collé, which consists of fitting fragments of real objects into paintings, from 1943 onwards Picasso tried to show that there is nothing which cannot be raised to the dignity of art. As an example we might take André Warnod's account of his visit to Picasso, when the artist showed him a metal statuette which looked just like a woman's form. As Warnod could not tell where it came from or judge its style, Picasso told him it was only a bit of his gas-stove. This would be nothing but a paradox if we did not know that the statuette of a Woman (page 234) is made of corrugated*

THE TOAD. 13 JANUARY 1(
LITHOGRAPH, 19$\frac{3}{4}$" × 2

as being completely abstract? Was he trying to qualify space in a new way, as is suggested by the lines running in every possible direction, oddly punctuated with dots or ending in little bulges or circles? He also used that calligraphic manner in a new series of *Seated Women*, even accentuating it by exaggerating the thickness of the lines and the knots, to the point of giving them the appearance of something like a coat-rack. The outlines of the face, the hair, the arms of the arm-chair are indicated by heavy strokes, sprouting occasionally into bulbous forms. In *The Seated Woman in a Blue Dress with White Spots* (1949) this mannerism has spread over the whole composition. It is not just the lines but the forms themselves that appear to be made up of knotted points. This picture is remarkable in other respects. Picasso obviously painted it, together with half a dozen others, by facing himself with the kind of problems that concerned Matisse. The interlocked arabesques, dry but vivid, clear-cut tones and purely decorative intention show that he was strongly stimulated by Matisse, whether he copied him or not. Matisse's style acted as a

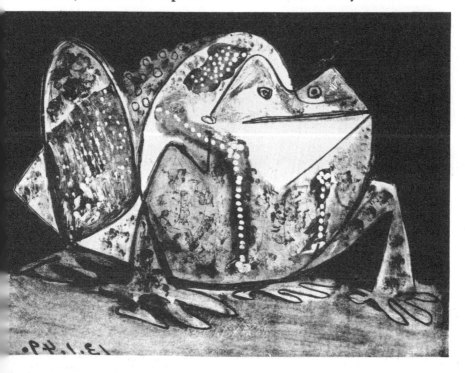

reagent on his own artistic investigations. The results prove nothing, except that Matisse remains Matisse and Picasso cannot be anything but Picasso, and that he is even more Picasso when he plays at being Matisse. There was no question of rivalry, but if we have to compare them, Matisse is an inimitable, incomparable master of colour, while Picasso has a better grasp of forms. What distinguishes him from the former Fauve, Matisse, is that the themes and elements of Picasso's work are never external to himself. He never paints a woman for the sake of the colour of her blouse or her dress, but because he cares for her, nor a thing or an animal for some aesthetic reason, but because he is emotionally attracted in some way. When a theme disappears from his paintings it is because he has had enough of it. The places where he lives or loves, or where his children are born also have claims on his sensibility. This is why in 1950 and 1951 the coast of southern France inspired him to make a few landscapes which are perhaps the most cheerful he ever painted. They usually show a farmstead among orange-trees and lemon-trees, the fruits glinting through the foliage. And then the series was sharply interrupted by the *Korean Massacres* (1951). This was a new protest against war, declamatory rather than just violent, and weakened by its reminiscences or its political intention. The *Dream and Lie of Franco* and *Guernica* came from the man's very

cardboard, a cake-tin and a motor-cycle petrol-tank; or that the Monkey *of 1952 is a construction made up of a child's ball, a frying-pan handle and two toy motor-cars joined together to form a head; or that the* Stork, *also of 1952, has an old fork for its foot, a navvy's spade for its wings, while its neck consists of a length of cable, and a gas-tap serves for its crest. The* Woman Reading *reproduced on page 230 is no less surprising. The limbs consist simply of nuts and bolts,*

the body is a piece of wood picked up on a vacant lot, and the fingers are five joiner's nails. Even more astonishing is the Goat, *the lower part of which is covered in places with plaster. This is a masterpiece of meticulous care and inventiveness. Its chest was made of a wicker basket, its dugs are two terra-cotta jars, while the spine is a palm-branch which has the advantage of both firmness and suppleness. A few nails, a few metal pipes, a few bits of old wood and a fruit-can were*

238

MOTHER AND CHILD. 1953 CONSTRUC
IN WOOD. HEIGHT ABOUT 80 INC
Artist's Colle

depths, but there is little of the heart in the *Korean Massacres*, and this tells on the execution.

Picasso was still at Vallauris when he made some of his most moving sculptures. Chief among them is the *Pregnant Woman* (1950) in which he has passed beyond realism and achieved that universality which primitive cultures expressed in their 'Earth-Mothers'. Another is *The Goat* (1950). He has taken up the eternal theme of fertility in this poor pregnant goat, which is sculpted with a ferocious energy, an almost cynical emphasis on truth. The animal is shown life-size, solidly planted on its hooves, with the bony structure almost sticking through the scarified surface of the bronze. While the head, neck, back and feet are little more than jagged lines and harsh intersecting planes, the belly and dugs are treated, on the other hand, with infinite delicacy. After this the sculptures were turned out rapidly in every dimension and medium: plaster, bronze, wood, ceramics. He continued bringing together all sorts of incongruous objects, saved from the dustbin by his mania for hoarding and collecting: an old flat-iron, an old mooring-ring, a fruit-tin. . . . He continued the series of 'owls', sculpted heads, feminine figures, an extraordinary *Monkey* and a *Crane* (1952), a *Woman Reading* in painted wood (1952), and, also in painted wood, a statue (6 ft 8 in. high) of a *Mother and Child* (1953). He was very interested in polychrome

all he required for holding this odd assortment together. These inventions which result from a genuine state of hallucination show Picasso's unusual sensitiveness to the compelling power of poetry. He said to Michel Leiris one day, "You should be able to pick up a piece of wood and find you have a bird in your hand."

In the summer of 1952 Picasso worked on the two panels, War and Peace. *These panels, specially designed for the walls of an abandoned chapel at Vallauris, were intended to be joined together in such a way as to form a vault in which the public could meet. For this work—the most ambitious work ever undertaken by the artist— between 28th April and 14th September 1952 he made no less than 150 drawings and sketches, the progress of which can be followed in a book published in 1954 by the 'Cercle d'Art' under the title* War and Peace.

First shown to the public in 1953,

LUNCHEON. VALLAURIS, 6 FEBRUARY 1953. OIL ON PLYWOOD, $39\frac{1}{4}'' \times 52''$. *Artist's Collection.*

*these panels formed the main attraction
of the two large Picasso exhibitions
held in Rome and Milan. They could
not be shown at the exhibition held at
the Musée des Arts Décoratifs from
1st June to 15th October 1955, as by
this time they had been installed in the
chapel for which they were intended.
This exhibition, completed by the one
held at the Bibliothèque Nationale
which showed his engravings, will be
known as one of those 'retrospectives'
that gave the public some insight into
a work which cannot easily be grasped*

*as a whole, thanks to the careful
choice and importance of the paintings
which were shown.*

*

*As we reach the end of this biogra-
phical outline, we are aware that if
we have sometimes been obliged only to
skirt certain essential events, it was
because any closer approach would
have yielded very little, and because it
is Picasso's work as a whole, in its
many phases and moods, which alone
can provide the best form of biography.*

sculpture after 1952, and to such an extent that he applied colour
even to his bronzes. He was perhaps the first to revive a process
which was used from early times until the Renaissance.

All these activities did not keep him from lithography. Between
1919 and 1930 he had already tried this technique, though with a
certain amount of caution, drawing with a lithographic pencil on to
paper which was subsequently transferred to the stone, or else
tracing his figures on to the stone. In 1945 he gave up etching and
threw himself enthusiastically into lithography, whose secrets he
soon mastered. For the next three years he was often to be seen at
Mourlot's workshop, or else in his own studio, engraving *corridas*
still-lifes, pastoral scenes, girls' faces, portraits of Françoise Gilot,
and doves and owls. When he had more experience he often used
wash and colour, and at times scoring, rubbing or superimpression.
What for others would be only refinements or tricks of the craft
became originality and an enrichment of the medium in his hands.
His lithographic output increased again in 1949. In that year he

ILYA EHRENBOURG. PENCIL.
WARSAW, 29 AUGUST 1948.

produced such staggering successes as *The Lobster*, *The Toad* and *Tropical Plants*. In 1951 he made a plate which is a masterpiece, *The Knight and the Page*, a new theme suggested by the illustrations in a copy of *Ivanhoe*, and which he treated in numerous drawings. The eighteen versions of *Two Nudes* (1946) and the eleven of *The Bull* (1946), with the nine of *David and Bathsheba* (1947–49) give us a clear insight into one of his methods of creation. He has several. Either he advances cautiously towards the aim he has in mind, or at a single stroke, with an impressively swift decisiveness, achieves it without further ado. Sometimes he works out a task with great care, gradually cutting out the superfluous or unnecessary details, simplifying his line, concentrating or increasing the density of his forms, and sometimes he seems to improvise, to produce at one blow some total statement which in reality had been gradually forming over a long period in his subconscious mind.

Since 1953 he has painted still-lifes, landscapes, 'Seated women' (such as the *Woman Seated in an Armchair*, March 1953), naturalistic portraits and some which are very freely interpreted, such as those of *Sylvette David* (1954). Shortly afterwards he was inspired to make

BALZAC. 25 NOVEMBER 1952.
LITHOGRAPH, 27¼″ × 20⅜″.

two superb portraits through his meeting Jacqueline R—— at Cannes. In the first of these the model is seen in profile, and in the other three-quarter face. In the first of these (page 250) the young woman has her arms gracefully round her knees, and is sitting on a black-tiled floor. The head rises straight from the shoulders on the long neck, and is drawn in firm strokes which bring out the self-willed and commanding expression. All the exposed parts are uniformly white, standing out against the blue and red background, while the yellow parallels in the dress help to define volume. Then in February 1955 Picasso finished a series of fourteen pictures based on Delacroix's *Algerian Women*. Delacroix's famous picture was for Picasso only a pretext for graphic and pictural variations which were of an entirely personal nature. This was not the first time that Picasso took up some old masterpiece and gave free rein to his own imagination, for purposes completely alien to those that the original painter had in mind. Five years earlier he had 'interpreted' El Greco's *Painter* as well as Courbet's *Young Women by the Seine*. He 'remade' them, not without a certain element of impertinence, using methods which El Greco and Courbet could not have even heard of and asserting his own principles above the established ones —that is to say, that in art there are no principles at all. When he allowed himself to make parodies of Poussin, Cranach and Delacroix, we may rest assured that it was not in order to learn from the old masters, but both to take up their researches and throw light on his own. It was with a kind of malicious pleasure that he took up some museum work, turned it over like an old coat, recut it and adjusted it to his own measurements.

Works as impressive as *Guernica* and *War and Peace* are sufficient evidence that Picasso's work can be recognized by an extreme sensitiveness to the events and struggles of his age. Painted in 1952 after hundreds of sketches and preparatory drawings, the two isorel panels of *War and Peace*, which both measure $15\frac{3}{4} \times 34$ ft, were designed for the walls of an unused chapel at Vallauris. This explains their

244

unusual size. On the first panel War is shown brandishing a blood-stained sword and advancing in the form of an odd, horned figure, standing in a hearse which is drawn by a few old nags. Peace, carrying the sword of justice and a pure untarnished shield, stands waiting for this miserable team to appear. In the background a group of soldiers are silhouetted, wielding their arms. The composition is full of symbols which explain the artist's intention. The colours are brighter than those generally used for frescoes: vermilion, blue, yellow, brown and white, with black predominating. A starless darkness seems to be falling on a scene played by ghosts. On the other panel of the diptych, *Peace*, it is blue, green and grey which create the desired atmosphere. Children are playing games, women dancing, a centaur is blowing into a reed pipe, a child leads a winged horse, and three people are quietly enjoying their leisure in the shade

of an orange-tree. Above this vision of a paradise on earth there hangs an enormous, multicoloured sun which looks down upon human happiness.

Much larger than *Guernica*, this diptych has neither its emotional violence nor masterly execution, nor that perfect adjustment between inspiration and expression which silenced the visitors to the Spanish pavilion at the 1937 Exhibition. It is true that colour, which was lacking from *Guernica*, was generously used in *War*, where, however, it tends to lessen the dramatic feeling because it distracts the senses. We are tempted to think that in 1952 Picasso was not in the same frame of mind as in 1937. Besides, if he seems to have been seeking to create something like naïve theatrical scenery and the attractions of the fair-ground so as to impress the crowd for whom *War and Peace* was designed, and if he deliberately used a curt and even trivial line and the garish colours so dear to the masses, and if he simplified and vulgarized his forms, the result was only to blunt the edge of his style. In spite of this, *War and Peace*, with its contrasts of dark and light, violence and serenity, is none the less a work of uncommon value. It is not meant just to please or to displease. It is conceived and executed without and against art, and is deliberately offered as something necessary. *War and Peace* was all the more necessary to Picasso himself as it freed him from one of his most deep-rooted obsessions. The urgent, painful theme it dealt with was handled less bitterly than in the *Korean Massacres*, which he painted in the following year. His heart had not cooled, nor was his inventive vein dried up, but other themes and obsessions were by now gripping and exciting him. Perhaps we should have another look at *War and Peace*. If War still appears on wings of darkness with its train of miseries and crimes, yet it already belongs to the past. It is withdrawing before its radiant opponent, who comes forward full of triumphant promises. This is no doubt how we must interpret the gesture of the Archangel, who stands fast, holding up the chariot of destruction and death with his shield, on which are emblazoned

246

Minerva and a symbolic dove. Peace is not confined to the panel named after it, but is seen also in the other, rising on the frontiers of hell to defy the bloodthirsty monster with unflinching courage. No, war no longer drove Picasso into that furious revolt and proud despair from which he had drawn such overwhelming effects in the past. Peace had entered into him, had found its way to his soul. Is some conversion on the way? To what feast will he invite us, on the shores of the hospitable Sirmio where the sea cast up a majestic divinity at his feet, in plumes of foam? Will he now openly enjoy the gifts of heaven and earth? Or else, too hardened a warrior, will this untirable conqueror set out in search of new spoils in a world which has already given him all it had to offer?

Reaching the end of this study we are fully aware of its faults. They are inevitable. We have taken the risk of wearying the reader in an attempt to keep track of an artist whose decisions are always

surprising and impossible to foresee, and to follow as closely as possible a career whose rapid, irregular and sometimes hidden progress can often elude the most careful observer. The reader could easily fall behind or find himself stuck in one of the many by-ways we have had to explore. This is why we have had to set up a few dates as milestones in Picasso's life, as well as adopting, against our own inclinations, the division of his work into 'periods' which we realize is both artificial and arbitrary. To clarify our work we have also had to make concessions to the mania for classifying and cataloguing which infects the abstract, logical era in which we live. But no creator is less amenable to such an analytical method of approach as Picasso, just as no work is harder than his to explain systematically. The so-called Blue, Pink, Negro, Cubist and Expressionist periods, dear to the critics, explain and mean nothing.

If we look back on his life and work, we see a painter who was not slow in showing his exceptional gifts, who soon shook off the academic canons, who was prodigal of his immense resources, who never once failed to assert his inventive powers, uncontrolled impulses, unbounded ambitions and flair for unlimited discovery, and who extended his prestige over reality, over men and success and everything except himself, and who now seems to have said everything and will yet have something more to say. His is an ever-changing, ever unforeseeable work. A burning confession, interrupted by sobs and derisive laughter, fury, caresses, insolence, witticisms and curses. Such is this capricious and fantastic artist, so changing and so contradictory that hardly has he finished a picture before he has begun another to deny it. No sooner has he finished a piece of sculpture, fired a piece of clay, traced out a drawing and dried a lithograph, than yet another work is there to confound us. New Picassos are always emerging, yet they are all equally impatient, restless, inconstant, proud, with a terrible vitality that can all be crammed into a terse drawing, or overflow into an avalanche or fill

RAIT OF MME JACQUELINE R———.
NE 1954. OIL, 46⅜" × 35⅝".
st's Collection.

the stage with grimacing figures, a crazy masquerade of shapes. Sometimes we find the snout of cruelty and stupidity lurking under some elegant disguise, or sweetness and compassion under the rags of a tumbler or a beggar. Anguish is dressed up as impudence, long-suffering as brutality, violence as seductiveness, doubt as certainty. When we are reduced to silence by the conjuror's tricks we cannot even see the emotion that unnerves his hand. The hoaxer's laugh drowns the cry of a wounded soul. It is when he is most generous with them that we think he is mean with his feelings, and when his heart seems hardened that he is most full of tenderness. We think he is cheating, just when he is giving himself completely; or cynical, when he is most trusting. He is taken for sincere when he is not, and for affected when he is being sincere; he side-steps when he is sought after and comes to meet you when you have turned your back, tricking us when we believe him and being honest when we think he is a trickster, and many a time tricking himself. He believes in nothing except, perhaps, mankind; he accepts nothing except what is thrust on him by surprise, his models and themes, his tools, the means and media that are given him by chance, by circumstances, by the passing moment. He is disconcerting in every aspect of his being. He seeks his inspiration in the real, or rather the real lays hold on his imagination, stirs it and gives it new life.

It is useless to try to ignore or conveniently put away such a turbulent and fearless personality as his. Some have tried to pigeon-hole him in conceptual categories or in the historian's card-index, but this cannot be done with so much passion, dreaming, invention, liveliness and colour in such a vast and many-sided output as his. Picasso never 'had the idea' of using only blue or pink rather than red or green. He never meddled with Cubism. "It was others who did that after him." It is only the learned commentators who claim that he painted cubes. They have been so successful in imposing their ideas that we have been obliged to follow them, for fear of not being followed in our turn. But there is no point in being taken in. No

DANCE OF THE BANDERILLAS. 14 FEBRUARY I
LITHOGRAPH, 20″ X

need to be like the Emperor, in that fable about the Chinese Nightingale, who preferred the mechanical bird to the real one. The real Picasso cannot be classified or easily summed up. We have only tried to draw nearer to him and take stock of the scandal of his genius. He can either in turn or simultaneously be romantic, classical, realist, unrealist, expressionist; he can respect nature or torture it, reproduce appearances or transform them into abstract signs, abase or exalt colour, stress modelling or relief then sharply replace them by line or flat colour. He can pass with ease from geometrical complexity to the simplest arabesque, express himself as well in a painting the size of a cathedral wall as in a two-minute sketch; he can please and displease, flatter or bully, charm and terrify, yet in spite of all these variations remain exactly the same person. For he does not contain several warring personalities. He is just an individualist who is interested in everything, in all the causes, forces and

PEACE. 1952. OIL,
PAINTED ON 'ISOREL', 188″ × 408″.
For a 'Temple of Peace' at Vallauris.

WAR. 1952. OIL,
PAINTED ON 'ISOREL', 188" × 408".
For a 'Temple of Peace' at Vallauris.

struggles on which the emotions feed and which he submits to his intellect. He is a lyricist ever anxious to renew himself and rediscover the universe, a revolutionary who pushes his inquiries in every direction, with no use for prejudices, opening doors on every hand and shutting them with a bang after him. He is an artist definable only by what separates him from others. A unique personality behind so many unresolved contradictions which he carries into his work, in which the peculiarities are very much those of his own temperament. We can only admire his vitality and his unrivalled ease of expression, the punch of his onslaughts, his flashing decision, the vigour of his line, which knows no rules, the boldness of his form, for ever new.

With whom can he be compared? To what line of ancestry does he belong? In spite of his Spanish origins we could as well relate him to the Greeks, the Italians or the African tribes, although he has spent most of his life in the land of Ingres and Delacroix. This Baroque luxuriance combined in his work with a classical severity, the provocative self-assurance shot through by qualms of anxiety, the mixture of aristocratic haughtiness and vulgar roughness of manner, the crude, materialistic realism sometimes transfigured by a kind of supernatural fire, such are the conflicting signs of a genuine creative urge. Creation finds itself in liberty, and this is a truth which nobody has more deeply felt or better illustrated than Picasso. His work reflects the misery of a modern world which has lost the consolation of Redemption, but it escapes from that world by freely creating another. He has a will to absolute creation and a will to absolute liberty: only the philosophers can explain the religious significance of these two aspects of the same principle.

If we are dismayed at the sight of so much energy, so many contrasts and exaggerations, perhaps it is because a Niagara has suddenly burst into the garden in which Art was a nice little elegant fountain. It is perhaps because we cling to the idea of the artist as a subtle, intelligent, delicate, clever, respectful heir to a tradition

STUDIO-SCENE. 21 JANUARY 195
WASH, 9⅝″ × 12⅜

and a long chain of masterpieces to which he was content if he could add a few small links. But as we have seen, Picasso has never worried about producing 'masterpieces', but rather aimed at shedding the visions and sensations by which he was obsessed, and at putting all he loved or hated into his pictures. As a sculptor he joins discarded odds and ends together. When he draws he does not mind what the size or quality of the paper is. He can paint quite happily on a dirty piece of cardboard, on a bit of warped wood, a rough-surfaced sheet of isorel or any old bit of canvas. He has little concern for the durability of his materials nor the help they can offer, and nothing stimulates him more than some such difficulty to be overcome. He refuses to bother with all the tedious business of making a good base or foundation which marks the good conscientious artisan, and makes light of such aspirations to immortality. He does not work for the museums and refuses to draw dud cheques on posthumous

6.4.49. VII

11-2-41 TOUT LE FATRAS IMMONDE DU TITAMARRE
DES LUMIÈRES AVEUGLANTES JETÉES SUR L'OCRE
PEINT DE LA FACE REMPLIE D'EXCREMENTS DE LA
CROSE CAISSE RESONNANTE DES NUAGES CRIANT
BLESSURE OUVERTE MONTRANT SES DENTS AU TROU
DU PUITS AGITANT SES AILES DECHIRÉES
LA GLACE DU MIROIR ENVELOPPANT LA CHAIR
QUI FOND DES OS PLANTÉS SUR
L'ARGILE ET LES CHEVEUX DEFAITS DE SES TRESSES
LEVANT LES BRAS LES MORCEAUX DES VITRES
BRISÉES COLLÉS AUX TEMPES DU TIC TAC DES
HORLOGES AGITÉES DES ALGUES ET LES
SOUPIRS ET LES RIDEAUX BATTUS PAR LES
COUPS AMOUREUX DES PARFUMS ET LES PLAINTES
DECHIRANTES DES FLEURS ECRASÉES SOUS LES ROUES
LES NAINS SÉPARANT L'EAU QUI SE DRESSE SUR
LA TABLE ET LA MUSIQUE CHIFFONNÉE DU LINGE
SONNANT A LA FENETRE SES SALUTS — RIEN QU'AU
SAUTS RIEN QU'A L'IMPERCEPTIBLE ODEUR DE SANTAL
DE SES DOIGTS MOUILLÉS RIEN QU'AU BRUIT FAIT
PAR SES CHEVEUX TAPANT SUR L'AIR LA PRESSION
DU COTON ET DE LA SOIE EVAPORANT DANS LA RONDE
DES OISEAUX MORTS DE CETTE APRES-MIDI LES
CHIENS DE MONTRE DE LA LUMIERE DU SOLEIL
MORDANT A L'EPAULE DU BUFFET LE CHAGRIN
ET LA RAGE QUI SE DETACHENT DU MUR RECOUVERT
DES RAMAGES BLEU CACA D'OIE ET AMARANTE
FONT LEUR CHOUX GRAS ET RECOLTENT RECOMPENSES

I

6.4.49. V

6.4.49. VI

fame. What matters for him is not what he does but what he is. He cares nothing for the approval of future generations, so long as he can be free now to carry human expression to a degree of incandescence that will make the Here and Now worth living in, without thought for the future. His greatness lies in this supreme unconcern about things that do not matter, and this awareness of himself and of his age. Picasso can be seen in all his authenticity in his assertion of the individual as he denounces the divine creation or accepts it in order to complete it, and in this search for the absolute in all created things. He might be called the man of the Eighth Day of creation.

A PAGE FROM 'POEMS AND LITHOGRAPHS' (1949–54). Text in Picasso's writing. *Published by the Louise Leiris Gallery.*

BIBLIOGRAPHY

CHRISTIAN ZERVOS: *Pablo Picasso*. 'Cahiers d'Art' publications. A monumental work of cataloguing which contains reproductions of all Picasso's paintings as well as a large number of drawings and most of the sculptures. *In course of publication*. Vol. I, *Œuvres* (Works) from 1895 to 1906 (1932); Vol. IIa, works from 1906 to 1912 (1942); Vol. IIb, works from 1912 to 1917 (1942); Vol. III, works from 1917 to 1919 (1949); Vol. IV, works from 1920 to 1922 (1951); Vol. V, works from 1923 to 1925 (1952); Vol. VI, supplement to the first five volumes; Vol. VII, works from 1926 to 1932 (1955).

BERNHARD GEISER: *Picasso, peintre-graveur*. Publ. by the author, Berne 1933, re-issued 1955. An illustrated catalogue of the engraved and lithographic works from 1899 to 1931, with 257 reproductions.

FERNAND MOURLOT: *Picasso lithographe*, with a Preface by Jaime Sabartés. Éditions du Livre, André Sauret, Monte-Carlo, 1949 and 1950. Two volumes, illustrated with all Picasso's lithographic work from 1919 to 1949.

DANIEL-HENRY KAHNWEILER: *Les sculptures de Picasso*. Éditions du Chêne, Paris 1949, 216 reproductions. English trans., Rodney Phillips & Co., London, 1949.

CH. ZERVOS, J. SABARTÉS, MADOURA: *Les céramiques de Picasso*. 'Cahiers d'Art', 23rd year, No. 1. Paris, 1948. 447 pieces illustrated.

JAIME SABARTÉS: *Picasso. Portraits et souvenirs*. Publ. by Louis Carré and Maximilien Vox, Paris, 1946.
— *Picasso, Documents iconographiques* (Picasso, a pictorial record). Publ. by Pierre Cailler, Geneva, 1954.

ALFRED H. BARR: *Picasso: Fifty Years of his Art*. Publ. by the Museum of Modern Art, New York, 1946.

J. BILBO: *Pablo Picasso: thirty important paintings*. M. RODRIGUEZ CODOLA: 'Exposición Ruiz Picasso,' *La Vanguardia*, Barcelona, 1897. MIGUEL UTRILLO (under the pseudonym, 'Pincell'). 'Pablo R Picasso,' In *Pél y ploma*, Barcelona, June 1901. F. FAGUS: 'L'invasion espagnole Picasso.' In *La Revue Blanche*, Paris, 1901. G. APOLLINAIRE. 'Picasso' In *La Plume*, Paris, May 1905. A SALMON: *La jeune peinture française*, Paris, 1912. G. STEIN: 'Pablo Picasso.' In *Camera Work*, special issue, 1912. G. APOLLINAIRE: *Les peintres cubistes*, Paris, 1913. D. H. KAHNWEILER: *Der Weg zum Kubismus*, Munich, 1920. M. RAYNAL: *Picasso*, Paris, 1921. J. COCTEAU: *Picasso*, Paris, 1923. P. REVERDY: *Pablo Picasso*, Paris, 1924. W. GEORGE: *Picasso: Dessins*, Paris, 1926. MAX JACOB: 'Souvenirs sur Picasso,' in *Cahiers d'Art*, Paris, 1927. W. UHDE: *Picasso et la tradition française*, Paris, 1928. A. LEVEL: *Picasso*, Paris, 1928. A. BRETON: *Le surréalisme et la peinture*, Paris, 1928. EUGENIO D'ORS: *Picasso*, Paris, 1930. L. ARAGON: *La peinture au défi*, Paris, 1930. H. MAHAUT: *Picasso*, Paris, 1930. *Catalogue* of the Picasso Exhibition at the G. Petit Gallery, Paris, June–July 1932. *Catalogue* of the Picasso Exhibition at the Zurich Kunsthaus, September–October 1932. CAHIERS D'ART: Nos 3–5 devoted to Picasso, Paris, 1932. F. OLIVIER: *Picasso et ses amis*, Paris, 1933. CAHIERS D'ART: Nos. 7–10 devoted to Picasso, Paris, 1935. G. BAZIN: 'Pablo Picasso.' In *Histoire de l'Art contemporaine: La peinture*, Paris, 1935. G. DE TORRE: *Picasso*, Madrid, 1936. GACETA DE ARTE: No. 37, devoted to Picasso, Teneriff, 1936. J. SABARTÉS: *Picasso*, Milan, 1937. J. CASSOU: *Picasso*, Paris, 1937. CAHIERS D'ART: Nos. 4–5 devoted to *Guernica*, Paris, 1937. G. STEIN: *Picasso*, Paris, 1938.

P. Haesaerts: *Picasso et le goût du paroxysme,* Antwerp–Amsterdam, 1938. Cahiers d'Art: Nos. 3–10 devoted to Picasso, Paris, 1938. J. Merli: *Picasso, el artista y la obra de nuestro tiempo,* Buenos Aires, 1942. R. Desnos: *Picasso 1939–1943,* Paris, 1943. E. Prampolini: *Picasso scultore,* Rome, 1943. P. Éluard: *A Pablo Picasso,* Paris, 1944. (Also publ. in London, 1947.) R. Gomez de la Serna: *Completa y veridica historia de Picasso y el cubismo,* Turin, 1945. A. Cirici Pellicer: *Picasso antes de Picasso,* Barcelona 1946. Also in French; Geneva, 1950. H. and S. Janis: *Picasso, the recent years, 1939–1945,* New York, 1946. J. Sabartés: *Picasso,* Paris, 1946. J. Larrea: *Picasso: Guernica,* New York, 1947. J. Sabartés and Paul Éluard: *Picasso, à Antibes,* Paris, 1948. S. and G. Ramié: *Céramiques de Picasso,* Geneva, 1948. D. Sutton: *Picasso. Époques bleue et rose,* Paris, 1948. T. Tzara: *Pablo Picasso,* Geneva, 1948. Verve: Vol. V, Nos. 19–20 devoted to *Picasso at Antibes,* Paris, 1948. J. Lassaigne: *Picasso,* Paris, 1949. Ch. Zervos: *Dessins de Picasso, 1892–1948,* Paris, 1949. J. Sabartés: *Picasso, an intimate portrait,* London, 1949. J. Bouret: *Picasso. Dessins,* Paris, 1950. A. Leclerc: *Picasso.* Reproductions, with introductory essay by A. Leclerc, London, 1949. Picasso: *Desire caught by the tail.* A play, illustrated, London, 1950. Cahiers d'Art: No. 2 devoted to Picasso's early years in Barcelona, Paris, 1950. A. Verdet: *L'Homme au mouton* [sic], Paris, 1951. Roland Penrose: *Homage to Picasso on his 70th Birthday.* Drawings and water-colour since 1893, London, 1951. A. Bertram (ed.): *Picasso.* The World's Masters, New York, 1951. M. Gieure: *Initiation à l'Œuvre de Picasso,* Paris 1951. A. Verdet: *Picasso au Musée d'Antibes,* Paris, 1951. Verve Vol. VII, Nos. 25–26 devoted to *Picasso a Vallauris,* Paris, 1951. P. Éluard: *Picasso Dessins,* Paris, 1952. Le Point: October 1952 special Picasso number, Mulhouse, 1952. W. S. Lieberman, *Picasso, blue and rose periods,* New York, 1952. H. Briffault (transl.): *Desire trapped by the tail:* New World Writing, No. 79, New York, 1952. A. Verdet: *La chèvre de Picasso,* Paris, 1952. Claude Roy: *La Guerre et la Paix,* Paris 1953. M. Raynal: *Picasso,* Geneva, 1953. Also in English, *Picasso, biographical and critical studies,* London, 1953. T. Tzara: *Picasso et la poésie,* Rome, 1953. J. Sabartés: *Picasso ceramista,* Milan, 1953. F. Russoli *Catalogue* of the Picasso Exhibition at Milan, Milan, 1953. *Catalogue* of the Exhibition at Lyons Museum, 1953. 'Du': No. 7 devoted to Picasso, Zurich, July 1954. Verve Vol. III, Nos. 29–30: a series of *180 drawings* by the artist, Paris, 1954. M. Jardot *Catalogue* of the Picasso Exhibition at the Musée des Arts Décoratifs, Paris. Paris, 1955. B. Geiser: *L'œuvre gravé de Picasso,* Lausanne, 1955. Vercors: *Picasso. Œuvres des Musées de Leningrad et de Moscou,* Paris, 1955. W. Boeck and J. Sabartés: *Picasso,* London, 1955. B. Geiser and H. Bolliger: *Picasso: 50 Years of his Graphic Art,* London, 1955.

WORKS BY PICASSO
IN EUROPEAN MUSEUMS

This list is no doubt incomplete, although it was made after careful inquiries at the various European museums. Wherever possible the titles follow those given (in the French) by Christian Zervos in his monumental catalogue of Picasso's work. In other cases we have accepted the titles used by the museums themselves. The term *oil* stands for works painted in oil paint on canvas; otherwise the necessary details are added. The height of the painting is always noted before its breadth. Readers might regret that this list was not supplemented by the very important list of over 150 works by Picasso which are now in American museums. But it would have been superfluous to reprint the very detailed descriptions made by Dorothy C. Miller and William S. Lieberman, which can be consulted at the end of Alfred H. Barr's *Picasso, Fifty Years of his Art.*

FRANCE

PARIS (Musée national d'Art Moderne)

Portrait of Gustave Coquiot (1901). Oil, 40"x32". Given by G. Coquiot.

The Glass (1914). Gouache, papier-collé on cardboard, 14³/8"x6". Purchased by French National Museums.

Still-life (1914). Oil, 32³/8"x30". Given by Raoul La Roche.

Still-life (1922). Oil, 29¹/4"x36³/4". Given by Raoul La Roche.

Woman's Head (1924). Oil, 26"x21³/4".

Still-life with Classical Head (1925). Oil, 38³/4"x52". Given by Paul Rosenberg.

The Milliner's Workshop (1926). Oil, 68³/4"x106". Given by the artist.

Woman's Torso (1929). Oil, 40"x32". Bequeathed by Maurice Meunier.

Still-life with Apple-Charlotte (1929). Oil, 28³/4"x26". Bequeathed by Maurice Meunier.

The Muse (1935). Oil, 52"x64³/4". Given by the artist.

Figure. Oil, 40"x32³/4". Given by the artist.

Still-life with Lemon and Two Oranges (1936). Oil, 21⁵/8"x26". Given by the artist.

Woman's Portrait (1938). Oil, 39¹/4"x31". Given by the artist.

Portrait of Nush Éluard (1941). Oil, 28³/4"x24". Given by Paul Éluard.

Reclining Nude with Musician, known as 'The Aubade' (1942). Oil, 78"x106". Given by the artist.

The Rocking-chair (1943). Oil, 64³/8"x52", Given by the artist.

Still-life with Cherries (1943). Oil, 21⁵/8"x32³/8". Given by the artist.

The Woman in Blue (1944) Oil, 52"x58³/4". Given by the artist.

The Enamel Pan (1945). Oil, 32³/4"x42". Given by the artist.

Ceramics: Vase with Dancing-girls (1950). 30³/8" high. Purchased by French National Museums.

Musée des Beaux-Arts de la Ville de Paris (Petit-Palais)

Evocation (1901). Oil, 58³/8"x35⁵/8". Given by Ambroise Vollard.

Drawing in Coloured Crayon (1901). Former H. Vinès Collection.

The Madman (1905). Bronze, 18¹/4" high.

Head of a Girl (1906). Bronze, 4³/4" high.

Girardin Collection

The Pigeon, with Peas (1912). Oil, 24"x21⁵/8".

Man's Head (1912). Oil, 24³/8"x15¹/4".

Ham and Bottle of Old Marc (1914). Oil, 21³/8"x14³/8".

Composition (1920). Oil, 10⁵/8"x8".

ANTIBES (Picasso Museum, Grimaldi Palace)

Seven fibro-cement panels, painted in oil:

'La Joie de vivre', a pastoral scene. 48"x100".

Ulysses and the Sirens. About 180"x120".

Still-life with Fish, Fruit-bowl and Ewer, 48"x104".

Faun Playing the Flute, 100"x48".

Young Faun, Dancing, 100"x48".

Centaur with Trident, 100"x48".

Recumbent Woman, 48"x100".

Seven plywood panels painted in oil:

The Goat. Oil and charcoal, 48"x60".

Still-life with Water-melon, 38"x70".

Still-life. Bottle, Sea-urchins, Fruit-dish with Three Apples on a Table, 34³/4"x84".

Still-life. Fruit-bowl with Grapes, Guitar, Plate and Two Apples on a Table, 38³/8"x70".

Reclining Woman, 34³/4"x84".

Crouching Woman, 66"x58³/8".

Still-life with Fish, Muraena, Octopus, Sea-urchin, 36"x50³/4".

Five wood panels painted in oil:

Woman with Sea-urchins, 47⁵/8"x32".

The Idle Fisherman, 37⁵/8"x32".

Seated Fisherman, 32³/4"x42³/4".

Owl on a Chair, with Sea-urchins, 32"x30".

Composition (Harmony in Grey), 37³/8"x36³/8".

Eight oil-paintings on canvas:

Eating Sea-urchins, 52³/8"x32³/8".

Lemon, Fish, Aubergine, 11¹/4"x16³/8".

Basket, Sea-urchins and Lamp, 14"x26".

Cuttle-fish, Lemon, Fish and Sea-urchins, 24"x29¹/4".

Vase with Foliage and Sea-urchins, 18"x15¹/4".

Fish and Lemon, 15¹/₄"x 22".
Lemon and Fish, 15¹/₄"x 22".
The Cuttle-fish, 13¹/₄"x18³/₈".

Paintings in Ripolin (enamel paint) on paper
(26³/₈"x 20³/₈"):
Study for a Ewer: Four Fauns' Heads; Two
Heads of Satyrs Playing the Double-
flute; Two Still-lifes with Fish; One
Composition.

Three charcoal-drawings, touched up with
white Ripolin:
Studies for Fauns' or Satyrs' Heads,
26³/₈"x 20³/₈".

About 30 drawings, either in graphite or
indian ink, on *Arches* paper,
26³/₈"x 20³/₈".

Two cement sculptures: Woman's Heads
(1932).

NOTE: All the paintings and drawings at
the Antibes Museum were made between September 1946 and January 1947.

CAGNES-SUR-MER (*Château-Musée*)
One ceramic piece: Vase with Dancing-girls
(1950). 30³/₈" high.

CARCASSONNE (*Musée de la ville*)
Head (1926-30?). Pencil, 32"x 24".

CASTRES (*Goya Museum*)
Portrait of a Child (1903). Graphite,
12³/₄"x 10³/₄".

CÉRET (*Municipal Museum*)
Still-life. Oil, 18³/₈"x 22". Given by the artist.
Ceramics: A jug 12³/₈" high; Three dishes
(with picador, Faun, dove); 30 cupels
(with *corrida* and *toreros* designs, 6³/₄"
diameter, all unique pieces). Given by
the artist.

GRENOBLE (*City Museum*)
Child with a Doll (about 1899). Oil on wood,
9⁵/₈"x 13¹/₄".
The Bowl of Fruit (about 1907). Water-
colour, 9⁵/₈"x 12³/₈".
Woman, Reading (1920). Oil, 40"x 36³/₈".
Naked Man, Profile. Graphite, 15⁵/₈"x 8".
Standing Nude (1945). Bronze, 5¹/₄" high.

Nude (1945). Bronze, 8³/₈" high.
Nude (1945). Bronze, 10³/₈" high.
Hand (1945). Bronze, 9⁵/₈" wide.

LYONS (*Musée des Beaux-Arts, Palais Saint-Pierre*)
The 'Catalan' Sideboard (1943). Oil,
32³/₈"x 40".
Ceramics: The Red Owl (1953). 21¹/₄" h

NICE (*Musée Masséna*)
Ceramics: Large vase. Height, 26³/₄";
width, 13¹/₄".

RHEIMS (*City Museum*)
The Railwayman (1901). Water-colour,
8³/₈"x 5".
Woman in a Large Hat (about 1900). Pe
and chalk, 8³/₄"x 5⁵/₈".

SAINT-DENIS (*Municipal Museum,*
The Dove of Peace (1950). Pencil,
16³/₈"x 28³/₈".
Henri Martin (1952). Pencil, 12¹/₄"x 8¹/₄
Christmas (1953). Gouache, 29¹/₄"x 23¹/₄
The Dove (1952). Lithograph, dedicate
Paul Éluard, 21¹/₄"x 30".

SAINT-ÉTIENNE (*Musée d'Art et d'Industrie*)
Still-life with Pot, Glass and Orange (19
Oil, 13¹/₄"x 16³/₈".
Ceramics: Dish showing 4 profiles (195(
Diameter 10⁵/₈". (Original piece.)
Provençal jug (1952).
Dish Decorated with a Goat's He
(1952).

VALLAURIS
The Man with a Lamb (1944). Bronze,
high.
War (1952). Oil on Isorel, 188"x 408".
Peace (1952). Oil on Isorel, 188"x 408".
(The last two works are in the dis
chapel, Vallauris.)

GERMANY
BREMEN (*Kunsthalle*)
Woman's Head (1949). Oil, 16³/₈"x 10³/₄"
Head, and Study of Hands. Indian ink,
6³/₈"x 4³/₈".

COLOGNE *(Wallraf-Richartz Museum)*
Head of a Woman, Reading (1953). Oil on
   wood, 18³/₈″x 15¹/₄″.
Goat's Skull (1952). Wash, 20¹/₄″x 26¹/₄″.
Ceramics: Oval dish with *corrida* design
   (1948).

DUSSELDORF *(Kunstsammlungen)*
Ceramics: Terra-cotta jug (1948).
   Dish with design of a coffee-pot and
   cup (1948).

STUTTGART *(Staatliche Kunstsammlungen)*
King Dagobert (1905). Pastel, 22″x 18″.
Woman with Bent Head (1906). Oil,
   20³/₈″x 15³/₄″.
Woman's Head, Profile and Front-view.
   Water-colour on brown paper,
   24³/₄″x 18⁵/₈″.
Seated Woman (1906-7). Charcoal, 19″x11³/₄″.

WUPPERTAL-BARMEN *(Städtisches
   Museum)*
The Man in a Cape (1899). Oil, 32³/₈″x 20⁵/₈″.
The Offering (1908). Wash on paper,
   18⁵/₈″x 20⁵/₈″.

AUSTRIA
VIENNA *(Albertina)*
Study of a Seated Man (about 1905). Indian
   ink, 12⁵/₈″x 9³/₈″.
Study of a Recumbent Woman, Legs Raised
   (about 1905). Indian ink, 9¹/₂″x 12³/₈″.
Oriental Dancing-girl (about 1905). Indian
   ink, 9³/₄″x 6³/₄″.
Cubist Head. Pencil, 25¹/₄″ 18¹/₄″.

BELGIUM
LIÈGE *(Musée des Beaux-Arts)*
The Soler Family's picnic (1903). Oil,
   60″x 80″.

DENMARK
COPENHAGEN *(Royal Fine-Arts Museum)*
Village Street (1905). Oil, 21⁵/₈″x 15³/₈″.
   Rump Collection.
Enlaced Nudes (1905). Gouache and water-
   colour on paper, 10¹/₂″x 8³/₈″. Jarl
   Collection.

SPAIN
BARCELONA *(Museum of Modern Art)*
Woman Wearing a Shawl (1899). Pastel,
   9¹/₄″x 10³/₈″.
The Divan (1899). Pastel, 10″x 11⁵/₈″.
Lola Picasso, the Artist's Sister (1899). Char-
   coal coloured with spirit, 19⁵/₈″x 11⁵/₈″.
Lovers in the Street (1900). Pastel, 23⁵/₈″x 14″.
The End of the 'Turn' (1900). Pastel,
   28³/₄″x 18³/₈″.
Woman at a Looking-glass (1900). Pastel,
   19¹/₄″x 21¹/₄″.
The Fortune-teller (1901). Pastel, 18³/₄″x 12″.
Waiting (1901). Oil, 27¹/₄″x 23¹/₄″.
Midget Danseuse (1901). Oil, 40″x 26″.
La desserte (1901). Oil, 24″x 32³/₈″.
Woman with a Love-lock *(Femme à la mèche)*.
   1903. Water-colour, 22″x 14³/₄″.
Woman, with Child wearing a Tucker (1903).
   Pastel, 18³/₈″x 16″.
Sebastian Junyer Vidal (1904). Water-colour,
   22″x 18³/₈″.
The Madman (1904). Water-colour, 34″x 14″.
Mme Canals (1905). Oil, 35¹/₄″x 27¹/₄″.
Harlequin (1917). Oil.
Woman, in the Street (1900). Pen and water-
   colour, 6³/₄″x 3⁵/₈″.
Man and Woman in Evening-dress (1900). Pen
   and water-colour, 6³/₄″x 4³/₈″.
Woman in Green (1900). Pen and water-
   colour, 6³/₄″x 4⁵/₈″.
Can-can Dancer (1900). Pen and water-
   colour, 6³/₄″x 4³/₈″.
Chanteuse, Standing (1900). Pastel, 8″x 5″.
Page of sketches: three studies of a woman,
   a glass, a bottle (1900). Pen and
   coloured crayons, 5¹/₄″x 10¹/₄″.
Page of sketches: four cabmen's heads, one cab
   (1900). Coloured crayons, 5¹/₄″x 10¹/₄″

Garriga Roig legacy:
'La Chata' - a standing Gitane (1899).
   Coloured crayons, 30³/₈″x 12⁵/₈″.
Pere Romeu. No date. Pen and coloured
   crayons, 7¹/₄″x 5¹/₄″.
Nude on a Bed: a Man sitting at her Feet.
   Pen and coloured crayons, 7″x 9¹/₄″.
Woman in Profile: studies of heads (about
   1904?). Wash, 7¹/₄″x 6³/₈″.

MADRID *(National Museum of Modern Art)*
Woman in Blue (1901). Oil, 54"x 40".

SITGES *('Cau Ferrat' Museum)*
Santiago Rusiñol legacy:
Bulls, Running. Pastel and gouache,
6^1/$_2$"x 12^1/$_4$".
Three Can-can Dancers. Coloured crayons,
7^3/$_4$"x 5^1/$_4$".
D. Paco and Family. Pen, coloured crayons,
8"x 5^1/$_4$".
Seated Woman, Drinking, and Woman Standing. Pen, coloured crayons,
8^1/$_4$"x 5^3/$_8$".
Two Women, Sitting. Coloured crayons,
8^1/$_4$"x 5^3/$_8$".
Two Women, Standing. Coloured crayons,
8^1/$_4$"x 5^3/$_8$".

GREAT BRITAIN
CAMBRIDGE *(Fitzwilliam Museum)*
Vase of Flowers. No date. Oil, 17^3/$_8$"x 15^5/$_8$".

GLASGOW *(Art Gallery and Museum)*
The Flower-seller (1901). Oil on cardboard,
21^1/$_4$"x 14^1/$_4$".

LONDON *(Tate Gallery)*
Flowers (1901). Oil, 26"x 19^5/$_8$".
Woman in a Shift *(La Femme en Chemise)*
(1904). Oil, 28^3/$_8$"x 24".
Youth with a Horse (1905). Gouache,
20"x 12^3/$_4$".
Female Bust (1909). Oil, 29^1/$_4$"x 24".
Seated Nude (late 1909-early 1910). Oil,
36^3/$_4$"x 29^1/$_4$".
Nude in a Red Armchair (1932). Oil,
52"x 38^3/$_4$".
The Big Cock *(Le grand coq)* (1932). Bronze,
26" high.

OXFORD *(Ashmolean Museum)*
The Blue Roofs (1901). Oil, 16"x 24".
Nude. Pencil and ink, 12"x 8^1/$_2$".

GREECE
ATHENS *(National Pinakothek)*
Figure (1939). "For the Greek people: a tribute from Picasso. Paris, May 1946".
Oil, 26^3/$_8$"x16". Given by the artist.

HOLLAND
AMSTERDAM *(Stedelijk Museum)*
Still-life with a Mandoline (1924). Oil,
38^3/$_4$"x 41^1/$_4$". Regnault Collection.
Interior (1934). Oil, 40"x 32^3/$_8$". Regnault Collection.
Head of a Girl (1940). Oil, 26^3/$_8$"x 20".
The Aubergine (1946). Oil on paper, 20"x 22"

OTTERLO *(Rijksmuseum Kroller-Muller)*
Dancing-girl (before 1900). Pastel,
14^1/$_4$"x 8^1/$_4$".
Box in a Theatre (before 1900). Pencil,
14^1/$_4$"x 8^1/$_4$". *(On the back of the
preceding item.)*
Portrait of a Youth (before 1900). Pencil,
14^1/$_2$"x 11^5/$_8$".
Portrait of a Woman (about 1900). Oil on
wood, 20^3/$_4$"x 13^1/$_4$".
Nude (1908). Gouache, 24^3/$_4$"x18^3/$_8$".
Violin (1911-12). Oil, 40"x 29^1/$_4$".
Guitar (1919). Oil and sand on canvas,
32^1/$_4$"x 17^3/$_4$".

IRELAND
DUBLIN *(Municipal Gallery of Modern Art)*
The Orchids (1934). Oil on cardboard,
10^5/$_8$"x 8^3/$_4$".

NORWAY
OSLO *(Nasjonalgalleriet)*
The Poor Family (1903). Oil, 32^5/$_8$"x 26^1/$_4$"
Guitar (1913). Oil, 29"x 24".
Composition (before 1915). Oil, 21^1/$_4$"x 16^3/$_4$".
Still-life (1927). Oil, 29^1/$_4$"x 36^3/$_4$".
Guitar on a Table, before a Window (1927)
Black and coloured pencils, 7^1/$_2$" wide

SWEDEN
GOTEBORG *(Konstmuseum)*
The Kiss (1907). Water-colour, 15"x 10^5/$_8$".
Family of Acrobats, with a Monkey (1905).
Gouache on cardboard, 41^5/$_8$"x 30".
Fernande Olivier (1905). Water-colour,
24^5/$_8$"x 19^1/$_4$".
The Straw Hat (1939). Oil, 18^3/$_8$"x 15^1/$_4$".
Sea-fruit (1946). Oil on cardboard,
20^5/$_8$"x 26^3/$_8$".

Still-life. Graphite, 18³/₈″× 24¹/₄″.
Woman's Head (1905). Bronze, 13³/₈″ high.

STOCKHOLM (Nationalmuseum)

St Anthony (before 1914). Water-colour, 24″× 18³/₈″.
The Guitar-player (1916). Oil and sand on canvas, 52″× 38³/₄″.
Woman with Blue Collarette (1941). Oil, 24³/₄″× 20″.
Nude (1945). Bronze, 9¹/₄″ high.
Nude, Standing (1948). Bronze, 9⁵/₈″ high.
Nude with Folded Arms (1948). Bronze, 10³/₈″ high.
Ceramics: a plate (1951).

SWITZERLAND

BASLE (Kunstmuseum)

The Two Brothers (1905). Oil, 56⁵/₈″× 38³/₄″.
Bowl of Fruit and Loaves on a Table (1908). Oil, 65⁵/₈″× 52⁷/₈″.
The *Torero* (1912). Oil, 54″× 32³/₄″.
The Occasional-table (1914). Oil, 52″× 35⁵/₈″
Woman with a Guitar (1914). Oil, 52¹/₄″× 36″.
The Guitar (1920). Oil, 26¹/₈″× 36⁷/₈″.
Glass, Bottle, Packet of Tobacco (1922). Oil, 13³/₈″× 16¹/₂″.
Harlequin (1923). Oil, 52″× 38³/₄″.
The Young Ladies by the Seine; after Courbet (1950). Oil on wood, 40″× 80″.
The Naked Porter. Ink-drawing, 6″× 3¹/₂″.
Nude, Arms Raised, Front View. Graphite, 6″× 3¹/₂″. (On reverse of preceding item.)
Nude, Front View, Leaning on her Elbow. Graphite, 6″× 2³/₄″.

WINTERTHUR (Kunstverein)

Head of a Madman (1905). Bronze, 16³/₈″ high.
One drawing.

ZURICH (Kunsthaus)

Acrobat, Sitting with a Boy (1906). Tempera on cardboard, 40″× 28″.
Female Bust (1907). Oil, 29⁵/₈″× 24″.*
Landscape (1908). Oil on wood, 26³/₄″× 9⁵/₈″.*

Woman in a Chemise, in an Armchair (1913). Oil, 60″× 40″.*
The Occasional-table. Oil, 53¹/₄″× 41⁵/₈″.
Guitar (1920). Oil, 35⁵/₈″× 46³/₈″.*
Piano. Gouache, 10³/₄″× 8³/₈″.*
Woman in a Chemise (1921). Oil, 46³/₈″× 29¹/₄″.*
Bowl of Fruit and Guitar (1921). Pastel and indian ink, 42³/₈″× 29⁵/₈″.*
Guitar, Glass and Fruit-dish, with Fruit (1924). Oil, 38³/₄″× 52″.
Man with a Guitar (about 1925). Water-colour, 12″× 9¹/₄″.*
Woman, Dressing (1917). Pencil on wood, 60″× 20³/₄″.*
The Dancing-girl (1917). Pencil on wood, 60″× 20³/₄″.*
Nude, Standing (1917). Pencil on wood, 60″× 20³/₄″.*
Still-life (1925). Pencil, 10³/₈″× 10″.*
Bowl of Fruit, Jug and Glass (about 1925). Indian ink, 18³/₄″× 25¹/₄″.*
Ecstasy (about 1943). Pen drawing, 13⁵/₈″× 10″.
Woman's Head (1909). Bronze, 16³/₈″ high.

U.S.S.R.

LENINGRAD (Hermitage Museum)

Woman Drinking Absinthe (Buveuse d'absinthe) (1901). Oil, 29¹/₄″× 21⁵/₈″.
The Interview (1902). Oil on wood, 60³/₄″× 40″.
Portrait of Soler (1903). Oil, 40″× 28″.
Woman's Head, with Kerchief (1903). Oil, 20″× 14³/₈″.
Boy with a Dog (1905). Gouache on cardboard, 22³/₈″× 16³/₈″.
The Naked Youth (1905). Indian ink and gouache on cardboard, 22³/₈″× 16³/₈″.
Still-life with Leeks (1905). Oil, 15¹/₄″× 22³/₈″.
Female Bust, Nude (1906-7). Oil, 24³/₈″× 18³/₄″.
The Dance of the Veils (1907). Oil, 60″× 40″.
Still-life with Death's-head (1907). Oil, 46″× 35¹/₄″.
Black Ice-pail with Green Tureen (1908). Oil, 24″× 19⁵/₈″.

* Held on loan to the museum from Frau Dr Ingeborg Eichmann.

Glass, Pot and Book (1908). Oil, 22"x 18³/₈".
Carafe and Three Basins (1908). Oil on cardboard, 26³/₈"x 20³/₈".
Small House in a Garden (Maisonette dans un jardin) (1908). Oil, 29¹/₄"x 24".
Bathing (1908). Oil, 15³/₈"x 25".
Friendship (1908). Oil, 60³/₄"x 40³/₈".
Seated Nude (1908). Oil, 60"x 40".
The Farmer's Wife (full length) (1908). Oil, 32³/₈"x 26".
The Farmer's Wife (bust) (1908). Oil, 32³/₈"x 26".
Nude in a Forest (1908). Oil, 74"x 43¹/₄".
Woman with a Fan (1908). Oil, 60"x 40".
Three Women (1908-9). Oil, 80"x 71⁵/₈".
Seated Nude (1908-9). Oil, 40"x 32³/₈".
Flowers in a Grey Vase, with a Glass (1908-9). Oil, 32³/₈"x 26".
Still-life: Fruit-dish, Fruit and Glass (1909). Oil, 36³/₈"x 29³/₈".
The Factory, Horta de Ebro (1909). Oil, 21¹/₄"x 24".
Woman with a Mandoline (1909). Oil, 36³/₄"x 29¹/₄".
Naked Man with Folded Arms. Gouache on paper, 25³/₈"x 19¹/₄".
Nude, Seated in an Armchair (1909-10). Oil, 36³/₄"x 29¹/₄".
Musical Instruments (1912-13). Oil and plaster on canvas, 39¹/₄"x 32".
Bottle of Pernod, with Glass (1912). Oil, 18¹/₄"x 13".
Violin and Glass (1912). Oil, 26"x 21⁵/₈".
Violin and Clarinet (1912). Oil, 22"x13¹/₄".
Fruit-dish with Bunch of Grapes (1914). Gouache, papier-collé and sawdust, 27³/₈"x 21¹/₄".
Composition: Bunch of Grapes and Sliced Pear (1914). Wallpaper, gouache and pencil, 14"x 12³/₄".
The Knuckle of Ham (1914). Oil and sawdust on cardboard, 11³/₄"x 15¹/₄" (oval).

MOSCOW *(Pushkin Museum of Decorative Arts)*

The Embrace (1900). Oil, 20³/₄"x 22¹/₄".
Harlequin and his Partner (1900). Oil, 28¹/₄"x 23³/₄".
Portrait of Jaime Sabartés, known as 'Le Bock' (1901). Oil, 32³/₈"x 26".
The Old Jew (1903). Oil, 50"x 36³/₄".
The Acrobat with a Ball. Oil, 58³/₈"x 38³/₄".
Old Man's Head, with Tiara (1905). Indian ink, 6³/₄"x 4".
Majorcan Woman (1905). Gouache and watercolour, 27¹/₄"x 20³/₄".
The Tumblers *(Les Bateleurs)* (1905). Charcoal and gouache, 20"x 24".
The Horse (1905). Indian ink, 8³/₈"x 10³/₄".
Study for the Still-life with Death's-head (1907). Water-colour, gouache and pencil, 12³/₄"x 9³/₈".
Study for 'Friendship' (1908). Water-colour and gouache, 24³/₈"x 18³/₄".
Study for 'Friendship' (1908). Water-colour and gouache, 24³/₈"x 18³/₄".
Small house and trees (1908). Oil, 36³/₄"x 29¹/₄".
Study for 'Three women' (1909). Water-colour and gouache, 21¹/₄"x 18³/₄".
Queen Isabeau (1909). Oil, 36³/₄"x 29¹/₄".
The Woman with the Fan (1909). Oil, 40³/₈"x 32³/₈".
Portrait of Ambroise Vollard (1901). Oil, 36³/₄"x 26".
The Oval Violin (1911-12). Oil, 22"x 18³/₈".

YUGOSLAVIA

BELGRADE *(National Museum)*

Woman's Head. (About 1910.) Oil, 23⁵/₈"x 20".
Three Female Figures, in an Interior (1926). Pen, 11³/₈"x 15".
Horseman (1928). Pen, 12³/₈"x 10³/₄".

CHRONOLOGICAL LIST
OF PRINCIPAL WORKS

While it is hardly necessary to stress the importance of this list, which gives 261 works by the artist running from 1894 to 1955, the reasons for our choice must be made clear. As the title shows, only the main works out of Picasso's immense output have been selected, due regard being paid to the need for absolute continuity in such a summary. Needless to say, the reader will find here all those canvases which have been analysed or mentioned in the text (apart from those already reproduced) in a chronological order allowing easy reference. The sub-titles are arranged in the following sequence: year; title of work; place of origin; exact date where possible; medium; dimensions (with the height always given before the width, as in the text).

1894–95. Man in a Cap.
Oil, 28³/₈″×19⁵/₈″.

Early 1895. Portrait of a Man.
Corunna. Oil, 19¹/₄″×12″.

1895. Barefooted Girl. Oil,
29¹/₂″×19⁵/₈″. Signature: P. Ruiz.

1897. Science and Charity.
Barcelona. Oil.

1900. The Embrace. Paris.
Oil, 20³/₄″×22¹/₄″.

1900. Harlequin with his Partner.
Paris. Oil, 28¹/₄″×23³/₄″.

1901. In the Café.
Pastel, 21⁵/₈″×29¹/₂″.

1901. Evocation. Paris.
Oil, 58³/₈″×35⁵/₈″.

1901. Dining out (Les Soupeurs).
Paris. Oil, 18³/₈″×24³/₈″.

1901. Harlequin. Paris.
Oil, 31^1/$_2$"×22^7/$_8$".

1901. Child with a Pigeon. Paris.
Oil, 29^1/$_4$"×21^5/$_8$".

1901. The Toilet. Paris (bd de Clichy).
Oil, 20"×24^3/$_8$".

1901. Gustave Coquiot. Paris. Oil.

1901. Maternity. Paris.
Oil, 36^3/$_4$"×24".

1901. Self-portrait. Paris.
Oil, 20^1/$_8$"×12^5/$_8$".

1901. Le Bock (Jaime Sabartés).
Paris (Autumn). Oil, 32^3/$_8$"×26".

1902. Women in a Bar. Barcelona.
Oil, 32"×36^3/$_4$".

1902. The Tippler. Barcelona.
Oil, 32"×24".

1902. Mother and Child. Oil.

1902–3. Madame Soler. Barcelona. Oil, 39$^1/_8$″ × 27$^5/_8$″.

1903. Angel Fernandez de Soto. Barcelona. Oil, 29$^5/_8$″ × 21$^1/_4$″.

1903. Life. Barcelona. Oil, 78″ × 52″.

1903. The Soler Family's Picnic. Barcelona. Oil, 60″ × 80″.

1903. Poor Folk by the Sea. Barcelona. Oil on wood, 42″ × 28″.

1903. Célestine. Barcelona. Oil, 32$^3/_8$″ × 24″.

1903. The Old Jew. Barcelona. Oil, 50″ × 36$^3/_4$″.

1903. The Embrace. Barcelona.
Pastel on cardboard, $39^1/_4'' \times 23^5/_8''$.

1904. Woman Ironing.
Barcelona. Oil, $46^1/_8'' \times 29^1/_8''$.

1904. Head of a Woman. Paris.
Gouache on cardboard, $16^3/_4'' \times 12''$.

1904. The Couple. Paris.
Oil, $40'' \times 32^3/_8''$.

1904. Harlequin's Death-bed. Paris.
Gouache on cardboard, $27^5/_8'' \times 38^3/_8''$.

1904. Woman wearing a Shift. Paris
Oil, $29'' \times 24''$.

1904. The Actor. Paris.
(Winter). Oil, $77^5/_8'' \times 44^3/_4''$.

1904. The Acrobat with a Ball.
Paris. Oil, $58/_8'' \times 28^3/_4''$.

1905. Family of Acrobats with a Monkey.
Paris. Gouache on cardboard, $41^5/_8'' \times 30''$.

1905. Acrobats with a Dog. Paris.
Gouache on cardboard, 42″ × 30″.

1905. Girl with a Basket of
Flowers. Paris. Oil, 60³/₄″ × 26″.

1905. Majorcan Woman. Gouache.

1905. Study for the Tumblers
(Les Bateleurs). Paris. Wash,
pastel and charcoal, 24″ × 18³/₄″.

1905. The Tumblers (Les Bateleurs). Paris.
Oil, 86″ × 91⁵/₈″.

1905. Naked Youth Leading a
Horse. Paris. Oil, 88″ × 52″.

1905–6. The Coiffure. Paris.
Oil, 70″ × 40″.

1906. Woman with a Loaf. Gosol
(Summer). Oil, 40″ × 28″.

1906. Fernande Olivier. Gosol
(Summer). Oil, 40″ × 32³/₈″.

1906. Gertrude Stein. Paris
(Autumn). Oil, 36″ × 32″.

1906 Portrait of the Artist.
Paris (Autumn). Oil, 36″ × 28″.

1906. Nude. $31^1/_2'' \times 25^1/_4''$.

1906–7. Study for 'The Young Ladies of Avignon'. Paris. Oil, $46^7/_8'' \times 36^5/_8''$.

1907. The 'Big Avignon Dancer'. Paris (Summer). Oil, $60'' \times 40''$.

1907. Flowers on a Table. Paris. (Summer). Oil, $36^3/_4'' \times 29^1/_4''$.

1907. Nude with a Towel. Paris (Winter). Oil, $46^1/_8'' \times 32^5/_8''$.

1908. Woman with a Fan. Paris (Summer). Oil, $60'' \times 40''$.

1908. Houses in a Garden. La-Rue-des-Bois (Autumn). Oil, $29^1/_4'' \times 24''$.

1908. Nude in a Forest. Paris (Winter). Oil, $74^3/_8'' \times 42^3/_4''$.

1908. Still-life with Loaves. Oil, $64^3/_4'' \times 52''$.

1908 9. Woman with Guitar. Oil.

1909. The Factory. Horta de Ebro (Summer). Oil, $21^1/_4'' \times 24''$.

1909. Portrait of Fernande. Horta de Ebro (Summer). Oil, $24^3/_8'' \times 20''$.

1909. Woman with a Mandoline.
Paris (Summer). Oil, 36³/₄″ × 29¹/₄″.

1909. Woman in Green. Paris
(Winter). Oil, 40″ × 32³/₈″.

1910. Girl with a Mandoline.
Paris. Oil, 40″ × 29¹/₄″.

1910. Wilhelm Uhde. Paris (Spring).
Oil, 32″ × 26″.

1910. Henry Kahnweiler. Paris
(Autumn). Oil, 40″ × 29¹/₄″.

1911. The Mandoline-player.
Paris (Spring). Oil, 40″ × 28″.

1911. The Accordion-player.
Céret (Summer). Oil, 52″ × 35⁵/₈″.

1911. Woman with a Guitar
(Ma Jolie). Paris (Winter). Oil, 40″ × 26″.

1912. Coquilles Saint-Jacques. Paris
(Spring). Oil, 15¹/₄″ × 22″.

1912. The Céret Fête. Paris
(Spring). Oil, 9⁵/₈″ × 16³/₈″.

1912. The Poet. Paris
(Spring). Oil, 24″ × 19¹/₄″.

1912. Violin, Glass, Pipe and Anchor.
Paris (Spring). Oil, 32¹/₈″ × 21⁵/₈″.

1912. The Violin (Jolie Eva).
Oil, 24″ × 32³/₈″.

1912. A Souvenir from Le Havre.
Paris (Autumn). Oil, 32³/₈″ × 21⁵/₈″.

1912. The Little Violin. Paris
(Winter). Oil, 14″ × 10³/₄″.

1912. Violin and Bowl of Fruit,
Paris (Winter). Gummed paper
and pastel, 26″ × 20″.

1912. The Bottle of Suze. Paris
(Winter). Gummed paper, 26″ × 20″.

1912–13. Violin Hanging on
the Wall. Paris. Oil, 26″ × 20″.

1913. At the 'Bon Marché'. Paris. Oil and gummed paper on cardboard, $9^5/_8'' \times 15^1/_4''$.

1913. Violin and Glass. Paris. Oil, $26'' \times 21^5/_8''$.

1913. Violin in a Café. Paris (Spring). Oil, $32^1/_8'' \times 21^5/_8$.

1913. Bottle of O'd Marc, with Glass and Newspaper. Paris. Gummed paper, $25^5/_8'' \times 20^1/_8''$.

1913. Woman in a Shift, in an Armchair. Paris (Winter). Oil, $59^1/_4'' \times 39^3/_8''$.

1914. The Card-player. Paris. Oil, $43^1/_4'' \times 35^3/_4''$.

1914. Man Smoking. Paris. Oil on canvas with gummed cloth, $55^1/_4'' \times 26^3/_8''$.

1914. Head. Paris. Gummed paper, $17^5/_8'' \times 13^5/_8''$.

1914. Pipe, Glass, Playing-card, Guitar and Dice. Paris. Oil, $18'' \times 16^1/_4''$.

1914. Portrait of a Girl, with Green Background. Avignon (Summer). Oil, 52″ × 31⁵/₈.

1914. Dice, Glass, Bottle of Bass, Playing-card, Visiting-card. Paris. Oil.

1915. Harlequin. Paris. Oil, 72³/₄″ × 42″.

1916. Man with Newspaper. Paris. Oil.

1917. Italian Woman. Rome. Oil.

1917. Drop-curtain for Parade. Montrouge (Paris). Oil.

1917. Guitar. Oil, 28³/₄″×24″.

1917. Mme Olga Picasso.
Oil, 48″×30″.

1918. Harlequin with Guitar. Paris.
Oil, 40″×32³/₈″.

1918. Mme Olga Picasso.
Oil, 52″×35³/₈″.

1918. Seated Pierrot. Paris.
Oil, 36³/₄″×29¹/₄″.

1918. Violin-player.
Oil, 56³/₄″×40″.

1919. Still-life on a Chest of
Drawers. Paris. Oil, 32³/₈″×40″.

1919. Still-life on Occasional-
table. Oil, 46³/₈″×29¹/₄″.

1920. Two Women. 28 April.
Oil, 26³/₈″×18⁷/₈″.

1920. The Bather. Paris.
Gouache, 10³/₄″×8³/₈″.

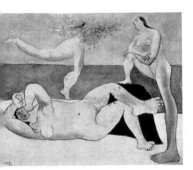

1920. Three Women Bathers. Juan-
les-Pins. Oil on wood, 32¹/₈″×40″.
(Wrongly dated 1923.)

1920. The Mantelpiece. Paris.
Pastel, 42″×30″.

1920. Two Seated Nudes. Paris.
Oil, 78″×75⁵/₈″.

1921. Guitar, Bottle and Fruit-dish.
Paris (10 April). Oil, 40″×36″.

1921. Girl in a Yellow Hat. Paris.
(16 April). Pastel, 42¹/₄″×30″.

1921. Four Women Bathers.
Tempera on wood, 4″×6″.

1921. Three Women at the Fountain,
Fontainebleau (Summer). Oil, 92″ × 66″.

1921. The Three Musicians. Fontainebleau
(Summer). Oil, 81¼″ × 75¼″.
(Philadelphia Museum of Art)

1921. Still-life with Loaf. Fontainebleau
(Summer). Oil, 40⅜″ × 51¼″.

1921. Maternity.
Oil, 64¼″ × 38¼″.

1921. The Woman in Blue.
Pastel, 42″ × 30″.

1921. Landscape. Oil.

1921. Mother and Child.
Oil, $38^3/_4'' \times 28^3/_8''$.

1921. The Spring. Oil, $26'' \times 36^1/_4''$.

1922. Still-life with Guitar. Oil, $33^1/_4'' \times 41''$.

1922. Mandoline on a Table. Paris.
Oil, $32^1/_8'' \times 40''$.

1922. Two Women Running on a Beach.
Gouache on wood, $13^1/_4'' \times 16^3/_8''$.
(Drop-curtain for 'The Blue Train', 1924.)

1922. Mother and Child.

1922–23. Still-life with Fish by the
Window. Dinard–Paris. Oil, $51^1/_8'' \times 38^1/_8''$.

1923. Bird-cage. Paris. Oil.
$78^3/_4'' \times 55^1/_8''$.

1923. The Artist's Mother. Cap
d'Antibes. Oil, $29^1/_4'' \times 24''$.

1923. The Lovers. Paris.
$52'' \times 32^3/_8''$.

1923. Harlequin with Clasped
Hands. Oil, $52'' \times 38^3/_4''$.

1923. The Painter Salvado, in
Harlequin's Costume. Paris.
Oil, $52'' \times 38^1/_4''$.

1923. Paul, the Artist's Son, Aged
Two, on a Donkey.
Oil, $40'' \times 32^3/_8''$.

1923. Picasso's Son, Paul, Aged
Two. Oil, 52″ × 38³/₄″.

1924. The Artist's Son, Aged Three,
in Harlequin's Costume.
Oil, 52″ × 38³/₄″.

1924. Mandoline and Guitar or The Open
Window. Juan-les-Pins. Oil, 57¹/₄″ × 80³/₄″.

1924. Harlequin with a Guitar.
Oil, 52″ × 38¹/₄″.

1924. The Musician's Table. Oil, 35⁷/₈″ × 44¹/₈″.

1924. Still-life with Guitar and
Fruit-bowl. Oil, 51¹/₈″ × 38¹/₈″.

1925. The Drawing-lesson.
Oil, 52″ × 38³/₄″.

1925. Dancing-girl with
Tambourine. Oil, 38³/₄″ × 52″.

1925. Statuary. Oil, 52″ × 38³/₄″.

1925. Still-life with Bottle of Wine. Oil, 38¹/₄″ × 52″.

1925. Still-life with Classical Head.
Oil, 38¹/₄″ × 52″.

1925. Still-life, Juan-les-Pins (Summer).
Oil with sand, 38¹/₈″ × 51¹/₈″.

1925. The Studio. Juan-les-Pins
(Summer). Oil, 38³/₄″ × 52″.

1925. Landscape. Juan-les-Pins
(Summer). Oil, 5⁵/₈″ × 22³/₄″.

1925. Caged Birds. Oil, 32³/₈″ × 40″.

1926. Still-life with Foliage. Oil.

1926. The Painter and his Model. Oil, 69¹/₄″ × 102″.

1927. Two Women at a Window. Oil, 38¹/₄″ × 52″.

1927. Harlequin as a Child.
Oil, 22″ × 18³/₄″.

1927–28. The Studio. Oil, 60″ × 92″.

1928. The Painter and his Model. Oil, 52″ × 64³/₄″.

1928. The Studio. Oil, 64³/₄″ × 52″.

1928. Bird on a Branch.
Dinard. Oil, 13³/₄″ × 9¹/₂″.

1928. Bathing-cabin. Dinard
(9 August). Oil, 14″ × 9⁵/₈″.

1928. Women Bathers on the Beach.
Dinard (12 August). Oil.

1928. Playing Ball. Dinard
(19 August). Oil, 7⁵/₈″ × 12³/₄″.

1928. Women Bathers with a Ball.
Dinard. Oil, 7¹/₂″ × 12³/₈″.

1928. Full-length Nude. Oil, 64³/₄″ × 52″.

1929. Woman Bather with Raised
Arms. Oil, 28³/₄″ × 23⁵/₈″.

1929. Woman Bather, Standing.
26 May. Oil, 78″ × 52″.

1929. Woman in a Red
Armchair. Oil, 26″ × 21⁵/₈″.

1929. Design for a Monument:
Womans' Head. Oil, 26″ × 21⁵/₈″.

1930. Woman Bather Seated by the Sea. January. Oil, 65¼″ × 52″.

1930. Figure. 4 January. Oil on wood, 25⅝″ × 18¾″.

1930. The Acrobat. 18 January. Oil, 64¾″ × 52″.

1930. The Painter. 20 January. Oil on wood, 20″ × 26″.

1931. Jug and Bowl of Fruit. 22 February. Oil, 52″ × 64¾″.

1931. The Red Armchair. 16 December. Oil and Ripolin paint on wood, 52″ × 38¾″.

1932. Woman Bather, Playing with a Ball. Oil, 58⅜″ × 45⅝″.

1932. Woman in an Armchair: The
Dream. Paris (24 January). Oil, 52″ × 38³/₄″.

1932. The Looking-glass. Paris
(12 March). Oil, 52″ × 38³/₄″.

1932. Young Woman with a Looking-
glass. Paris (14 March). Oil, 64″ × 52″.

1932. Woman with a Flower.
10 April. Oil, 54³/₄″ × 52″.

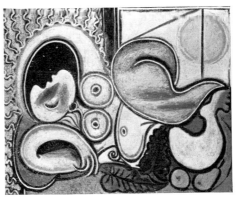

1932. Woman in a Red Armchair.
Oil, 51¹/₈″ × 38¹/₈″.

1932. Recumbent Woman. Oil and
Ripolin, 52″ × 64³/₄″.

1932. Nude with Sculptor's Turn-
table. Oil, 64³/₄″ × 52″.

1932. Recumbent Nude. Oil.

1932. Nude with a Necklace.
Oil, 36³/₄″ × 29¹/₄″.

1932. The Rescue.
Oil, 14″ × 10³/₄″.

1934. Two Girls, Reading. Boisgeloup (28 March). Oil, 36³/₄″ × 29¹/₄″.

1934. Bull-fight. Boisgeloup (22 July).
Oil, 38³/₄″ × 52″.

1934. Bull-fight. Boisgeloup. Oil, 20″ × 26″.

1935. Interior with Girl Drawing.
Paris (12 February). Oil, 52″ × 77⅝″.

1935. Girl, Reading. Oil and Ripolin,
64¾″ × 52″.

1937. Woman in a Yellow Jersey.
Oil, 25⅝″ × 21¼″.

1937. Woman Seated on the Beach. 10 February.
Oil and charcoal, 52″ × 64¾″.

1937. Seated Woman, Holding a
Book. Oil and Conté, 52″ × 38¾″.

1937. Portrait of Mlle Dora
Maar. Oil, 36″ × 26″·

1937. Boats on the Shore. Juan-les-
Pins (13 August). Oil, 15¼″ × 18⅜″.

1937. Weeping Woman. Paris
(26 October). Oil, 24″ × 19⁵/₈″.

1938. Portrait of Maya Picasso,
Aged 2¹/₂. 16 January. Oil, 29¹/₄″ × 24″.

1938. Man with a Lollipop.
20 August. Oil, 27¹/₄″ × 17⁵/₈″.

1938. Seated Woman. Oil, 64⁵/₄″ × 52″.

1938. Still-life with Black Bull's Head. Oil, 26″ × 21⁵/₈″.

1939. Woman Wearing a Hat.
7 April. Oil, 26″ × 21⁵/₈″.

1939. Cat with a Bird. 22 April.
Oil, 32³/₈″ × 40″.

1939. Seated Woman, Wearing a
Hat. 30 November. Oil, 36″ × 24³/₈″.

1939. Woman Dressing her
Hair. Royan (30 December).
Gouache, 18³/₄″ × 15¹/₄″.

1940. Nude, Dressing her Hair.
Royan (dated 6 March but
painted in June). Oil, 52″ × 38³/₄″.

1940. Conger-eels. Royan (27 March).
Oil, 29¹/₄″ × 36³/₄″.

1940. Seated Woman with
Green Bodice. 11 April.
Oil, 29¹/₄″ × 21⁵/₈″.

1941. Nude. Paris.
Oil, 36³/₄″ × 26″.

1941. Seated Woman with
Blue Bodice. Paris (8 June).
Oil, 36³/₄″ × 24″.

1941. Portrait of Nush Éluard.
Paris (19 August). Oil, 28³/₄″ × 24″.

1941. Woman in an Armchair.
Paris (19 June). Oil, 51¹/₈″ × 36¹/₈″.

1941. Woman in an Armchair.
Oil.

1941–42. Woman Seated in an Armchair. Paris. O 1, 52″ × 38³/₄″.

1942. Woman's Head. Paris (12 January) Oil, 16¹/₄″ × 12″

1942. Seated Woman with Fish-hat. Paris (19 April). Oil, 40″ × 32³/₈″.

1942. Reclining Nude with Musician: the Aubade. Paris (4 May). Oil, 78″ × 106″.

1942. Still-life with Pigeon. Paris. Oil, 24″ × 29¹/₄″.

1942. Still-life with Ox-skull. Paris. Oil, 52″ × 38³/₄″.

1942. Still-life with Guitar. Paris Oil, 40″ × 32³/₈″.

1942. Woman with an Artichoke. Paris. Oil, 78″ × 52″.

1942. Still-life with Eggs. Paris
(12 August). Oil, 35⅝″ × 46⅜″.

1942. Recumbent Nude. Paris (30 September).
Oil, 52″ × 78″.

1942. Still-life with Woman's Bust.
Paris. Oil, 40″ × 32⅜″.

1943. Woman with Striped Bodice.
Paris (20 September). Oil, 40″ × 32⅜″.

1943. Woman in a Wicker Chair.
Paris (24 September). Oil, 40″ × 32⅜″.

1943. Woman's Bust with
Yellow Bodice. Paris.
Gummed paper, 26″ × 20″.

1943. The Rocking-chair. Paris.
Oil, 64⅜″ × 52″.

1944. Seated Woman in Blue. Paris.
Oil, 52″ × 38¾″.

1944. Still-life with Candle. Paris (4 April).
Oil, 24″ × 36³/₄″.

1944. The Tomato-plant. Paris
(3 August). Oil, 29¹/₄″ × 36³/₄″.

1945. The Enamel Pan. Paris
(16 February). Oil, 32³/₄″ × 42″.

1945. The Charnel-house. Paris (Summer).
Oil, 80″ × 100″.

1945. Still-life with Death's Head
and Leeks. Oil, 32³/₈″ × 46³/₈″.

1946. View of Ménerbes. Ménerbes
(13 July). Gouache, 13¹/₄″ × 20¹/₄″.

1946. Pastoral. Ménerbes (22 July).
Gouache, 20³/₈″ × 26″.

1946. The Faun in Purple
Tights. Antibes (2 September).
Ripolin on paper, 26³/₈″ × 20³/₈″.

1946. Faun. Playing Pipes.
Antibes (14 October).
Ripolin on paper, 26³/₈″ × 20³/₈″.

1946. Sea-urchins. Antibes.
(21 October). Ripolin on paper,
20³/₈″ × 26³/₈″.

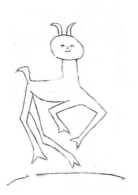

1946. Faun, Playing the
Flute. Antibes (Autumn). Oil
on fibro-cement, 100″ × 48″.

1946. Young Faun, Dancing.
Antibes (Autumn) Oil on
fibro-cement, 100″ × 48″.

1946. Centaur with Trident.
Antibes (Autumn). Oil on
fibro-cement, 100″ × 48″.

1946. Still-life with Water-melon.
Antibes (Autumn). Oil on plywood, 38″ × 70″.

1946. Still-life with Fish, Fruit-bowl and Ewer.
Antibes (Autumn). Oil on fibro-cement, 48″ × 104″.

1946. La Joie de Vivre: a Pastoral Scene. Antibes (Autumn).
Oil on fibro-cement, 48″ × 100″.

1946. Owl on a Chair, with
Sea-urchins. Antibes (Autumn).
Oil on plywood, 32″ × 30″.

1946. The Idle Fisherman. Antibes
(Autumn). Oil on plywood, 37⅝″ × 32″.

1946. Recumbent Woman. Antibes (Autumn).
Oil on fibro-cement, 48″ × 100″.

1946. Reclining Woman. Antibes (Autumn).
Oil on plywood, 48″ × 102″.

1946. The Goat. Antibes (Autumn).
Oil and charcoal on plywood, 48″ × 60″.

1948. The Kitchen. Oil, 70″ × 100″.

1948. Seated Woman.
Oil, 36³/₄″ × 29¹/₄″.

1948. Claude, Picasso's Son, Aged
Eighteen Months, in his Cot.
Oil, 52″ × 38³/₄″.

1948. Claude in
Polish Costume.
Oil, 48³/₈″ × 20″.

1948. Lobster and Bottle.
26 December. Oil, 20″ × 24³/₈″.

1949. Seated Woman. Paris
(23 March). Oil, 40″ × 32³/₈″.

1950. Claude and Paloma. Vallauris
(20 January). Oil and Ripolin on
plywood, 46³/₈″ × 35⁵/₈″.

1950. Winter Landscape. Vallauris
(22 December). Oil, 40³/₈″ × 49⁵/₈″.

1951. Paloma. Vallauris
(7 January). Oil, 10³/₄″ × 8³/₄″.

1951. Smoking Chimneys. Vallauris
(12 January). Oil, 24″ × 29¹/₄″.

1951. The Korean Massacres. Vallauris (18 January).
Oil on plywood, 44″ × 84″.

1952. Paloma, Asleep. Vallauris.
Oil on plywood, 45⁵/₈″ × 58³/₈″.

1952. Goat's Skull, Bottle and
Candle. Oil, 35⁵/₈″ × 46³/₈″.

1952. Mediterranean Landscape. Vallauris
(10 September). Ripolin on Isorel, 32³/₈″ × 50″.

1952. The Reservoir. Vallauris.
Oil on Isorel, 32″ × 49⅝″.

1952. Portrait of Hélène Parmelin.
Oil and Ripolin on plywood,
58⅜″ × 38⅜″.

1953. Seated Woman. 31 March.
Oil, 18⅜″ × 15¼″.

953. Female Torso. Vallauris
(17 July). Oil on plywood,
35¼″ × 28¾″.

1953. Reading (with Red Background). Ripolin on plywood, 32⅜″ × 40″.

1954. Portrait of Sylvette, in a Green
Armchair. Vallauris Oil, 32⅜″ × 26″.

1954. Portrait of Sylvette.
Vallauris. Oil, 46″ × 36″.

1955. The Algerian Women. Paris (14 February).
Oil ,45⅝″ × 58⅜″.

1905 André Salmon. *Poèmes*. One dry-point. Vers et Prose, Paris.

1911 Max Jacob. *Saint Matorel*. 4 etchings. Kahnweiler, Paris.

1914 M. Jacob. *Le siège de Jérusalem*. 3 etchings and aquatints. Kahnweiler, Paris.

1914 M. Jacob. *Le cornet à dés*. One line-engraving. Publ. by the author, Paris.

1918 M. Jacob. *Le phanérogame*. One etching. Publ. by the author, Paris.

1919 M. Jacob. *La défense de Tartuffe*. One line-engraving. Publ. by the author, Paris.

1921 Paul Valéry. *La Jeune Parque*. One lithographic transfer. N.R.F., Paris.

1922 Pierre Reverdy. *Cravates de chanvre*. 3 etchings. Nord-Sud, Paris.

1923 André Breton. *Clair de terre*. One dry-point. Publ. by the author, Paris.

1926 Waldemar George. *Picasso, dessins*. One lithograph. Édit. des Quatre Chemins, Paris.

1926 Christian Zervos. *Picasso. Œuvres 1920–1926*. One etching. Les Cahiers d'Art, Paris.

1928 André Level. *Picasso*. One lithograph. Crès, Paris.

1929 *Le Manuscrit autographe*, No. 21. One lithograph. Auguste Blaizot, Paris.

1930 Eugenio d'Ors. *Pablo Picasso*. One lithograph. Chroniques du Jour, Paris.

1931 H. de Balzac. *Le chef-d'œuvre inconnu*. 13 etchings and 67 drawings by the artist, wood engravings by Aubert. Vollard, Paris.

1931 Ovid. *Les métamorphoses*. 30 etchings. Skira, Lausanne.

1933 Tristan Tzara. *L'Antitête*. One etching. Les Cahiers Libres, Paris.

1934 Aristophanes. *Lysistrata*. 6 etchings. Limited Editions Club, New York.

1934 Georges Hugnet. *Petite anthologie poétique du Surréalisme*. One etching. Éditions Surréalistes, Paris.

1934 Benjamin Péret. *De derrière les fagots*. One etching. Éditions Surréalistes, Paris.

1936 Paul Éluard: *La barre d'appui*. 3 etchings. Les Cahiers d'Art, Paris.

1936 Paul Éluard. *Les yeux fertiles*. One etching. G.L.M., Paris.

1937 Pablo Picasso. *Sueño y mentira de Franco*. 2 large aquatint plates, each containing 9 scenes of the Spanish civil war, Paris.

1938 Luc Decaunes. *L'Indicatif présent ou l'Infirme tel qu'il est*. One etching. Soutes, Paris.

1938 Paul Éluard. *Solidarité*. One etching. G.L.M., Paris.

1939 *Hommage à la Tchécoslovaquie*. With texts by Langer, Claudel and Valéry. One lino-cut. Publ. by Les Artistes Tchécoslovaques, Paris.

1940 A. Breton. *Anthologie de l'humour noir*. One etching. Le Sagittaire, Paris.

1940 Iliazd. *Afat*. 6 engravings. Publ. by the author, Paris.

1940 Pierre Mabille. *Le miroir du Merveilleux*. One etching. Le Sagittaire, Paris.

1941 Paul Éluard. *Poèmes du 'Livre ouvert'*. 15 manuscript copies, each of 20 pages, and each page illustrated with original drawings by Picasso. Publ. by the author, Paris.

1942 Buffon. *Histoire naturelle*. 31 aquatints. Fabiani, Paris.

1942 G. Hugnet. *Non-vouloir*. 4 engravings. Robert-J. Godet, Paris.

1943 G. Hugnet. *La chèvre-feuille*. 6 engravings. Robert-J. Godet, Paris.

1944 Robert Desnos. *Contrée*. One etching. Les Trois Collines, Geneva.

1944 P. Éluard. *Au rendez-vous allemand*. One etching. Édit. de Minuit, Paris.

1945 René Char. *Le marteau sans maître*. One dry-point. José Corti, Paris.

1947 A. Gleizes and Metzinger. *Du Cubisme*. One etching. Paris.

1947 Petrarch. *Cinq sonnets*. One etching. Édit. 'A la Fontaine de Vaucluse', Paris.

1947 Ramón Reventos. *Dos contes*. 4 etchings. Albor, Paris-Barcelona.

1947 Ramón Reventos. *Deux contes*. French edn. 4 new etchings. Albor, Paris.

1948 Gongora. *Vingt poèmes.* 41 etchings, with the Spanish text engraved by the artist. 'Les grands Peintres modernes et le Livre', Paris.

1948 Iliazd. *Escrito.* 6 etchings. Publ. by the author, Paris.

1948 Ivan Goran Kovaćić. *La fosse commune.* One dry-point. La Bibliothèque française, Paris.

1948 P. Reverdy. *Le chant des morts.* 126 lithographs. Tériade, Paris.

1949 Ivan Goll. *Elégie d'Iphétonga.* Édit. 'Hémisphères', Paris.

1949 Iliazd. *Poésie de mots inconnus.* 2 lithographs and 1 dry-point. Publ. by the author, Paris.

1949 Prosper Mérimée. *Carmen.* 38 line-engravings and 4 aquatints. 'La Bibliothèque française', Paris.

1950 Aimé Césaire. *Corps perdu.* 32 engravings. Fragrance, Paris.

1950 Robert J. Godet. *L'âge du soleil.* One etching and one dry-point. Publ. by the author. Paris.

1950 Tristan Tzara. *De mémoire d'homme.* 9 lithographs. Bordas, Paris.

1951 Paul Éluard. *Le visage de la Paix.* 29 drawings and 1 lithograph. Publ. by Le Cercle d'Art, Paris.

1951 Valentine Penrose. *Dons des Féminines.* One etching. Les Pas Perdus, Paris.

1952 Adrian de Monluc. *La Maigre.* 10 dry-points. 'Degré 41', Paris.

1953 Maurice Toesca. *Six contes fantasques.* 6 line-engravings. Flammarion. Paris.

1954 Boris Kochno and Maria Luz. *Le Ballet.* One coloured lithograph. Hachette, Paris.

1954 Claude Roy. *La Guerre et la Paix.* One lithograph. Publ. by Le Cercle d'Art, Paris.

INDEX